The Warm Air Rises Too

Andrew Therriault

First Copyright © 2021 by Andrew Therriault
Second Copyright © 2025 by Andrew Therriault
All rights reserved. This book or any portion thereof
may not be reproduced or used in any manner whatsoever
without the express written permission of the publisher
except for the use of brief quotations in a book review.

Printed in the United States of America

ISBN 979-8-9941035-1-7

The Warm Air Rises Too

Chapter 1

Memory consists of everything, and beyond that is anything; all that I remember is light. It is mysterious to me, and that memory could have been my first week, first month, first year on earth. Whatever occurred before or after those first breaths, first steps—perhaps a relay of consciousness—this far back in memory and I am already lost if I try to take count of chronology. The light, I think, began toward the end of gestation. And that signified the beginning. I even took my first breath amid light—in light of the complications during childbirth. The umbilical was tangled around me, and right after that I developed asthma during infancy.

When light appeared at last, it flashed like lightning. It is hard to tell if these are my first memories—I remember doing this occasionally during infancy—having vivid, almost lucid dreams of landscapes, cityscapes, and seascapes. The dreams that I had in the early days, some of which are still clear to me now, had animals on land, fish underwater, streets and roads, trees and grass, kids and adults. The little boy that I was naturally revitalized myself. In the front yard under the oak tree, I dozed off after the journey. I was in bed dreaming of a dream. Other times, it was being highly moved by watching lightning and hearing thunder. Those instances are quite vivid. Back then, I may not have dreamt of writing this book when I first started it, or any book; just that I could write, and to write of the light, of all that comes from the stream of consciousness is how to write. I must have realized innately that it is a beneficial undertaking, to work hard at, progress, stylize, refine—something. Until then, I dreamt and dreamt between bouts of misfortune and fun, excursions, experiences and emotions through the course of growth and development.

I will soft-pedal some of the pains and misfortunes in this book. That was all under the surface, like the sound of lightning. In some dreams or reveries, I remember flashes of lightning frozen in the setting, immense storms, dark skies, and when bolts of light went far and wide, the clouds glowed mauve, a funnel suddenly formed overhead, the rain poured, hail bounced, and I flashed awake. I was fascinated by tornadoes and at first frightened by lightning, then enthralled and thrilled by the sound of thunder— the speed of sound and of light. I have never experienced a tornado, but I vividly remember many streaks of lightning and the light emitted, their erratic courses flowing through the surrounding sky as bolts but flashing in an instant, one second, maybe two, or three, and the sound of Earth releasing electric energy followed, radiating throughout the atmosphere toward the observer.

The summer months were warm. It was the first summer that I remembered. My family was having a little gathering at the house with my mother's relatives. We had had a few before then, earlier that year, when I met everyone and we celebrated. I may have still been crawling. I moved fast. I tumbled and rolled. I took my first step. Then I quickly became much more agile, but only when I needed to be. The day of this gathering was humid, the skies were hazy. Sunlight shone through the window wan. A rectangle of light appeared on the floor divided into segments. I lay prone in the living room on the carpet. I was warm in the light, I liked the light, I felt good. There was movement all around, feet, legs, and people. I studied them as they mingled together.

My brother Nico sat down. "What are you doing?" he asked.

"Nothing," I said.

"We're about to eat."

"Okay."

"We're having lasagna."

"I want dessert."

I got up and went into the kitchen. There were several bakery boxes on the counter. I wondered, pie, cake, cookies? I wished to see what was inside. Then, standing on my toes, I tried to reach the nearest box. I stretched, jumped and touched the box but pushed it further back on the counter. My grandmother walked over. She smiled. Her cheeks were round and rosy.

"What are you up to?" she asked. "It's not dessert time yet…"

"Yes," I said.

"You're just like your grandfather, Papa."

I jumped again and reached for the box. I came closer to it. I practically felt it. My grandmother opened the box and took out a pastry.

"Do you know what this is?" she asked.

"A cannoli," I said.

"Very good!"

My mother walked over. "Dessert already!"

"It's okay," said my grandmother. "He can have a cannoli."

"All right... Just one. I don't want you to spoil your appetite."

My grandmother handed me the cannolo. It was moist, fresh from the kitchen. The filling was warm and on either end the crust was covered in chocolate chips. I took a bite out of one side.

"What do you say?" said my mother.

"Thanks, Nana." I walked toward the basement, opened the door, flicked the light switch. I went slowly down the steps, and with one hand I held the railing and with the other the cannolo.

"Make sure he doesn't fall down those stairs," said my grandmother.

But I was focused. I was moving slowly down the stairs, and cautiously. To me as a young child, I was off on a small but seemingly colossal adventure. Something so simple as going down in the basement to explore the same ground as the day before seemed exciting. No one else in the house went into the basement often. It was a space to play in and explore. I had toys down there, small trucks, blocks, trains, and train tracks. Every day I made something new, did something different, formed some association of the world. I made it to the bottom of the stairs and ate the cannolo. The open space was empty and enormous. There were cardboard boxes piled high along the wall. I opened a box and looked inside, then opened another and looked again. The boxes were all empty, but I was searching for something. I traced the cracks in the concrete wall with my fingertip. Then I looked up at the small window and the sky and the sunlight streaming through the trees outside. Light, bright green leaves fluttered softly. I stood watching their movement for a moment, a slight pain in my abdomen.

Then, "Andrew, dinner is ready!"

I rushed over to the staircase, and using my arms and legs to climb faster, I went up the stairs like an animal. The grownups and my brother were in the kitchen filling their plates with lasagna, meatballs, sauce, pasta, bruschetta. In a bowl off to the side was a big salad. My mother liked to eat vegetables, but no one else in the house did at that time. She said, "I have your plate right here, Andrew."

"Okay," I said. "One minute." Then I got up from the table and walked to the door and went outside. First, I went through the garage between both parked cars. My mother drove a sedan, and my father drove a compact car. I looked at the scratch that I had made on his passenger door while I was on my scooter. He was not happy about it.

Outside in the sun, I brightened up a bit, and my mind was stimulated. I always walked around or played in the front yard. From there, the house seemed huge, though on the inside it was modest in size: three bedrooms, two and a half bathrooms. I stopped and looked at my neighbor's house across the street. The front wall was made almost entirely out of stone. I remembered how the stones felt playing yard games—cool and refreshing. I smiled and walked across the driveway and went into the patch of woods off to the side of the property, separating my other neighbor's house from ours. That was my spot, that patch of woods. I had poked a stick in the ground to make a sundial, and I made sure that it was still standing upright. That spot was my three-year-old world in the spring, summer, and fall. I wandered between trees, thinking about the outside world and everything within it. Who is God? Or, what else is up in the sky? Can I reach for the sun, the stars at night what is up in the tree? I started climbing trees when I was young, maybe just after I learned to walk. There was one tree that I favored to climb, and once toward the top, I heard my father say, "Hey, get down from there!" I climbed down and walked up to him. "There was a fisher cat in the tree," he said.

"Okay." I wondered, will a fisher cat eat me? My mother often tickled my belly, then said, "I could eat you right up!" But will the cat also make me laugh?

Remembering this excited me, so I went off exploring. Then a cheer arose from my neighbor's backyard. I thought that they were probably having a party too. But I could not see. There was a fence standing in the way, and inside that was a pool. My neighbors across the street had a trampoline. But I was still a young child. "Next summer," my mother said. "Your brain is developing."

I left my spot in the woods and began searching the lawn for a four-leaf clover. There were many three-leaf clovers, most of them clumped together. I examined each one in the ground. The sun grew dim, or it was going down, but I never looked up. The three-leaf clovers were self-similar; I may have already come across fractals in nature. There were so many of them. I brushed my hand along the grass very calmly, very slowly and smoothly, tickling my palm, hoping that a clover with four leaves would appear in my hand. Then it did. Just right in the middle of my palm. I held it lightly by the stem. I lifted my head toward the sky. Clouds had rolled in, and all around it had darkened. The wind picked up. The trees shook, and the leaves were silver, showing their undersides. I heard a faint rumble far off in the distance. Across the street the sky was dark grey. A storm was coming in from the lakes. Thunder, I thought. The sound of lightning. Then I went inside.

A few people were still eating at the table. Others were in the living room watching TV. They were all mingling, and then the door slammed shut from the wind behind me.

"There he is!" my father said.

I walked up to my grandmother. "Here Nana," I said.

"What is it, Andrew? Nice, a four-leaf clover."

"*Aw.*"

"You keep it," said my grandmother. "That's your clover."

"Okay," I said.

Then the storm was overhead. The lights inside were on. Outside it was gloomy. The rain clattered against the sides of the house, the roof, and on the deck like the sound of marbles falling on the floor, and it was exciting.

"What's that?" I asked.

"It's hailing," they told me.

Then there was the crack of lightning, clap of thunder. And then another that shook the house and sent me straight into my mother's arms. My face nestled in the corner between her neck and her shoulder. "It's just thunder," she said.

There were a few more flashes of lightning and an increasing interval between those and the sounds that they produced. Then someone said, "Look, the sun's coming back out."

I turned around. The light outside seemed golden. People were lining up in the kitchen. "Who wants tea?" A couple old ladies said, "Me!" Plates were filled with cuts of pie, pieces of cake, ice cream, whipped cream, and if there was still room, pastries. Then, as the tea kettle whistled, my great aunt started singing, "Tea for two, two for tea. Just me for you, and you for me." She had a voice that fit the song. It was harmonious until my brother began imitating her, and then I thought that it was ridiculous. An old lady singing that tune seemed all right, but not my brother. I walked off, holding my clover in one hand and my dessert plate in the other. I climbed the stairs and went into my bedroom. While eating dessert, the excitement over tea calmed down, and I joined the others at the table with my plate of lasagna. It was still light out, and the summer solstice got closer and the daylight hours a bit longer every day.

Chapter 2

We visited my grandparents several times during the summer. They lived fifteen minutes away in a nice neighborhood somewhat like mine. Playing outside at their house was a new world to me. There was a school next to their house at the end of the street and another school down the road from that. Behind their house and separated by a small patch of woods was a strip mall. Their front yard was boarded with shrubs, and there were flowers in a garden bed along the edge of their house that interested me. I examined each flower in depth. Sometimes, crawling on a leaf, I found a ladybug. Those insects were the most intriguing part of my study then because of the spots that dotted their shells. I thought that they were fun, and they could fly. Unlike flies or mosquitos, ladybugs were quiet and peaceful. One crawled slowly on a leaf. I let it crawl onto my fingertip. I went inside to show my grandmother. "Look, Nana."

"You have a ladybug." She smiled. "Ladybugs are good."

"Yes," I said.

"Go back outside now." She looked through the kitchen window. "Can you hear the birds?"

"Yes." I turned around and opened the door.

"Be gentle with the ladybug," she said.

Outside I returned the ladybug to the flower on which I had found it. The bug was still for a moment, then moved toward the grasshopper. I went off to explore the woods. There were some oak trees, birch trees, beech trees, and maple trees. On the ground were many leaves. Everything seemed vast, similar, defined, and fresh. When something new is taken in, absorbed, explored, it can feel magical.

I noticed a little trail. I followed it to the other side. It led to a parking lot beside the strip mall. I walked toward the closest store. Then someone came up to me. I had never seen him before but felt like I had. He had a big collection of baseball cards, apparently, and big blue eyes. I thought about my baseball cards. "Excuse me," I said.

I went back and found the trail. Walking through the woods, I listened to the birds. The sun was out, the air was warm, and the chickadees were singing.

"Chicka dee dee dee dee…" they called. "Chicka dee dee dee dee."

The bird's melody chimed all day in me.

I wandered off the trail and watched them fly and perch and fly again through the canopy. Once they found a branch to land on, they sang. Other birds sang too. It sounded like, "*Andrew. Andrew.*"

I sat on the ground in the leaves and lay back, looking up. The highest branches moved reposefully. The sky was clear and blue. The crescent moon was in sight. I could have stayed and watched the day turn to night. But then I heard my name in fact being called. My mother was outside looking for me.

"Andrew," she said.

I stood up and walked over to her.

"There you are! Come on, I want to show you where I went to school as a little girl."

"Okay," I said.

She took me by the hand and led me onto a paved pathway behind a fence. There was a softball field to the left and ahead stood a large brick building. We followed the pathway along the side of the building and behind it were tennis courts, basketball courts, softball fields, and two baseball diamonds. We walked through a parking lot and straight ahead was another brick building. "That's Hymie Lore," said my mother. "I went to school there when I was about your age."

I looked around and spotted a playground, a brand-new swing set, fresh woodchips. "I want to go for a swing," I said.

As we walked to the playground my mother told me about her former teachers and the sports that she had played. Tennis was her favorite sport, and one teacher, Mrs. Lambertson, was apparently only eight years old.

"How?" I asked.

"She was born on a leap year day!"

"What's that?"

"Well. Your birthday is in February, right? Do you remember how many days are usually in February?"

"No."

"That's okay." She smiled. "Every four years February has an extra day. Those years are special, they're called leap years. Usually February only has 28 days, but on a leap year, February has 29 days."

I figured it out.

"Mrs. Lambertson was born on a leap year, on February 29, and her birthday happened only once every four years. I was older than she was!"

"That's not fair," I said.

"She was a character."

I thought of an eccentric woman, maybe just from memory, with pink glasses.

On the swing, I swung as high as it could go. I pumped my legs in rhythm with the pendulated motion and toward the top of the swing the chains slacked. For a moment I felt weightless. That might be the bird's sensation in flight. I thought, how good they sing. And their tune started up again. I was very happy. My mother could tell.

"Smile," she said. "Show me those dimples."

I smiled, and then she laughed.

"There's a nice playground at the school you'll be going to. Does that sound good or what?"

"I'm not going to school," I told her.

"All the big kids go to school. You want to be a big kid, right?"

"Yes," I said.

"Well, you still have another year. Preschool will get you ready for school."

Chapter 3

Summer ended, and my parents had enrolled me in preschool. It was inside someone's house. Ms. Annesley was the teacher, and it must have been her house. The classroom that we used had once been a living room, she told us. That's why it was furnished. She had added the bookshelves and books and tables and games and chairs after she decided to run a preschool. The house was very big, but we were not supposed to go outside of the little classroom. We often went outside the house to play games in the yard. Inside, we played in the little classroom. Some of us were playing hide-and-seek once, and I went to the staircase and was going up the stairs when Ms. Annesley found me. She played a lot of games with us. Kids were often put into time-out. There were at least a dozen kids at the preschool, but I mostly played with Clyde, Avery, Chris, and Colson.

The five of us sometimes wrestled and fought, but it was for fun. We mainly tried to get more boys to wrestle with us. Or, if it was a quiet day, we tried to get them to play board games with us. The girls watched us, or they played their own games. Someone in our group went up to a boy in the corner a few times, then asked, "What are you reading, Clyde?" And if Clyde said, "*Dr. Seuss*" or any other book from the shelf: "Come wrestle with us, Clyde!"

"Clyde! Come wrestle with us!"

But Clyde kept reading. He was brought to all those places in Dr. Seuss's oeuvre. He must have liked them, the places, and the books. The rest of us carried on roughhousing, and then I started reading.

Ms. Annesley sometimes baked treats for us. She made cookies most often. I liked the chocolate chip cookies, but only when I dipped the cookies into milk. Sometimes she went to the store and bought us assorted donuts instead, and if anyone fought over a flavor, she looked the other way. Clyde was upset one time, holding his strawberry frosted donut between a paper towel. I said, "Here, Clyde, want to trade?" I held out my glazed donut. He grabbed it. He gave me his, and we ate at a table.

Then one of the girls brought a cake for her birthday. Ms. Annesley cut it into pieces, then she set each piece on a plate and handed out plates to everyone. We all sang happy birthday. I began eating. Then, a minute later, our teacher was calling first responders. There was peanut butter in the cake, or some other type of tree nut, and Clyde was allergic to tree nuts. He was swollen. I heard loud sirens outside and watched two first responders approach the door. They talked with our teacher, as Clyde was hoisted onto a stretcher, and then he went off in the ambulance. We all got to leave early that day.

Then, another day just after the school year began, we also got to leave early. All the mothers came and picked up their kids. All at the same time. Ms. Annesley's driveway was full of cars. Everyone was in a rush. "Come on," my mother said. "We have to go get your brother."

She and all the other grownups seemed very serious. I had a sense that something was wrong. I was quiet. The date was 9/11/2001.

We drove quickly down the street to the elementary school. The broadcasters on the radio spoke gravely. There were no open parking spots at the school. The place was crowded. We pulled up to the curb near the entrance. "Can I wait in the car?" I asked.

"No. Let's go get your brother."

My mother stepped outside and slammed the door. Her face was stern. She opened my door, unbuckled my seatbelt, and took me by the hand. "Come on."

Everyone rushed about, some frantically and full of energy. I did not know what was happening. It seemed as though, I thought, that I was brought into a bigger world. That the world must be big, and it's chaotic.

Chapter 4

There was a sense of angst for a period after that, and it was a time of distress, but I was not old enough to grasp it all. The kids still played as usual. Once domestic affairs seemed to be normal and broadcasters a bit more at ease, I went to a nearby zoo with Colson and his brother. Their mother brought us, and I thought that she was nice. Her long hair excited me. Colson's brother had a rattail. Along the nape of his neck, hair grew down on either side toward the center where it was thickest, sort of like a rat's tail. I was bemused by it at first, then amused and even charmed, almost as though it was a ponytail.

We bounced around the zoo from exhibit to exhibit. We saw kangaroos, camels, alligators, monkeys, owls, zebras. There was an enclosed area with many butterflies. And outside, somewhere around the corner, there was a big bird with fine legs, and it strut when it walked, it had a beautiful neck and big feathers colored green and blue with full-orbed spots that spread softly from its rear like a hand fan. I was hypnotized.

There were also some rides in the park. We went on a Ferris wheel, a carousel, a roller coaster, and then we raced down a big slide on some sheets of cloth. There were trees all around the park. It had plenty of autumn shade. I felt a light breeze, smelled the ocean air. After a little while I was hungry. My mother had given me a five-dollar bill to buy some lunch. I bought Dippin' Dots instead. I liked the cookie flavor. The other boys got French fries. Ian's brother wanted to do a trade with me.

"I'll give you a French fry for some of your Dippin' Dots."

"Okay," I said.

I gave him my cup of ice cream and he held out his basket of French fries. "The ones without ketchup I haven't eaten."

I took a few of the plain French fries and ate them.

"Hey, I said *a* French fry."

"Can I have my Dippin' Dots back?"

He scooped out a big spoonful and ate it. "This is pretty good. I don't think I've had this flavor."

"Yes you have," said Colson.

He had another big spoonful, and then he gave the cup back to me. There was much less inside than I remembered. And the spoon was all sticky.

He turned and walked up to his mother, and there it was again. He turned back, and then it was gone.

"Sorry about that," said Colson.

"That's okay."

We all decided to play miniature golf. There was a course in the middle of the park. I was good, but I often did unusual strokes and tricks whenever I putted, like ricocheting the ball off the walls or obstacles, as though I was playing billiards. Sometimes I even got a hole-in-one. This time I was a more disciplined with my play, for Colson's mother. I did well, but sometimes I got distracted by his brother's rattail. I had seen a few before, though never one that big. I thought that it was extraordinary.

After finishing the round, Ian's mother tallied our scores. She played golf, and she won. I had a good time, at the zoo, and playing miniature golf. Then we went back to the other end of the amusement park. We stopped at a popular exhibit. It was a large and open space with many trees and shaded areas, patches of grass and rocks to climb, a small pond and smaller pools of water.

I said, "Look, a lion!"

Colson and his brother turned around. I pulled on the rattail.

"Hey," he said. "What was that for?"

"Huh?" asked Colson.

"Why'd you do that?"

"Do what," said Colson.

We went on. Colson's brother asked about going to the gift shop. His mother said, "Sure." And then she bought him a baseball cap and shirt from the store. He wore both souvenirs for the rest of the day. Then, just before leaving the park, we all got our pictures taken. We stood before a wall of rock, the four of us, with a colorful parrot perched on wood above our heads. I held their mother's hand and felt good. I smiled big. She drove us back to the house. Then I ate dinner. It had been a thrilling day.

Chapter 5

Everyone on my mother's side of the family who lived close came to the house for Thanksgiving. We had a wonderful meal. My father cooked the turkey in a deep fryer, and it was delicious. I ate a lot. Everyone enjoyed the food. The turkey was a big success. So were the mashed potatoes, the gravy, the stuffing, and the cranberry sauce. When it was time for dessert, my great aunt sang her song and then drank a cup of tea. I ate my grandmother's homemade cherry pie and that was sweet and tart, rich and filling. My mother had dressed me in a festive sweater. The material felt coarse. I took the sweater off and put on an undershirt, eager to go to bed early. The day passed, then the week, then December came, and then it snowed. After that, I was inside most of the time, except for playing outside on the banks by the cul-de-sac and along the driveway.

That year we spent the holidays in Florida with my father's side of the family. We celebrated Christmas twice, once on Christmas day with my father's side of the family and also at grandparents' house on my mother's side of the family before leaving. I enjoyed their house more in the summer, though it was cozy during the holidays. The Christmas tree glowed incandescent and vibrant and smelled of fresh pine. There were presents underneath, stockings along the fireplace mantle.

My aunt Gina got me a toy bank, and the grownups had hidden some cash throughout the house to find and put in the bank. That's what I did most of the day. And I stood by the fireplace, smelling the Christmas tree pine and feeling the hot, incandescent light bulbs, intrigued by the star set atop the tree.

I went around the house with my bank. My brother went around with me. He said, "You're getting warmer;" or, after going past one of the gifts, "You're getting colder." It happened whenever I was getting closer to or further away from the funds. Then I collected them. I went into the living room. Everyone was having desert, pastries or tea.

"Hey Andrew."

"Hi."

"Did you find any presents?"

My math was slow.

"Fifty dollars," I said.

"Fifty dollars!"

My grandfather stood up. He pulled out a big wad of money from his pocket and peeled off the first bill. "Here, Vinny. Have this."

"Thank you, Papa," I said.

"Vinny?" My mother laughed. "Dad, that's Andrew."

"Who's Vinny?"

"I don't know."

"Jerry, sit back down," said my grandmother.

My grandfather sat in his chair. I liked the name Vinny that instance. I was quite excited from Christmas.

Someone had told me earlier about their love story. That he and my grandmother had met after church one day. She was walking on the sidewalk. It was just another Sunday. But he saw her and pulled up to the curb in his car. Asked if she needed a ride home, and she did. He was fourteen years older than she was. Two years later they married. I thought that it was great, interesting, exciting. And what a Sunday.

Later that night as we were getting ready to leave my grandparents' house, after I had played a few rounds of darts in their basement, from the kitchen I heard my grandmother say, "Jerry! Are you sleeping again?"

My parents laughed.

"You need to say goodbye to your grandchildren."

I rushed upstairs into the living room. My grandfather was indeed sleeping in his chair. I thought that he was a beautiful man. He was a veteran of the Second World War and the Korean War; an Italian, and one of my favorite elder grownups.

A few days later we flew to Florida. I saw everyone on my father's side of the family. Some of them I met just then for the first time. I had seen my father's parents often because they lived only about an hour away. My father's father was also one of my favorite elder grownups. I called him Pepa, and often he scratched my back. That usually happened as I watched television at his house. My parents and my grandmother thought that it was nice. Movies were my favorite kind of filming to watch on TV, most of the time, but especially as Pepa scratched my back. I thought that the movies were entertaining and that there were many genres. I liked love movies, but not necessarily the romantic type. My mother said that I was too young to be watching rated R movies. But the cable networks made them more suitable for kids.

In Florida, we only watched Christmas movies. That's really all I watched the whole month of December. Even in the airport, there were Christmas movies playing on TVs. Once our flight landed and we stepped outside, not only the climate felt different, but like it was an incredible kind of Christmas. At the house, it was winter. Then, it was amazing. It already seemed like a vacation on vacation just after a couple of minutes. I thought of playing outside, running around, learning to swim, and then I did.

First, we went to the condo and then unpacked our bags. The relatives were already there. We greeted each other. I said hello to everyone. It was mostly my aunts and uncles and my grandparents. My mother led me into a room where the kids slept. It was a big room with beds and furniture. My cousin Kelsey was sitting on the couch. I had seen girls at preschool before. But Kelsey was blonde. I felt like doing a somersault, head over heels, immediately. Then my mother said, "Go give your cousin a kiss."

I went up to her. I greeted her affectionately. She smiled. "Sit down," she said. I sat on the couch. We waited for my parents to unpack and for everyone to settle in.

Even though we had taken an early flight that morning, I had a lot of energy. I wanted to go to the pool, and then I asked my cousin Kyle if he could teach me how to swim. He said sure. Then we all went to the pool, everyone in the condo. We were the only ones at the pool then. Learning to swim was like learning how to ride a bike. It was pretty easy. I had fallen a few times while learning to ride a bike, but I only got a few scrapes on my elbow. In the pool, I started in the shallow end, and then after learning how to flutter my legs and move my hands and arms in the proper motion, I swam all around the pool. It seemed inborn or innate, like maybe humans had been aquatic creatures, first as microorganisms and then organisms, then evolved as complex organisms on land.

After a while, I got out of the pool. Almost everyone had already gone back to the condo, except for my brother, my mother, and me. He liked the water also, and she enjoyed being outside in the sun.

We were all festive. We watched *National Lampoon's Christmas Vacation* at least once. My father and his brother are identical twins. As we watched the movie, though they did not look like the father in the movie, Clark, to me they were both Clark. My mother and my aunt were both Clark's wife. Kids were the kids, and grandparents were the grandparents. It took some creativity to see everyone in the family as a character in *Christmas Vacation*, except for my aunt Brenda and uncle Scott. They were Clark's neighbors. The way Brenda said, "Scott!" and he said, "What!" thrilled me in a way the *National Lampoon's* movies did.

There was my cousin Mitch. He was about a year old and constantly grumpy that week. I thought that he was funny. He liked chocolate-frosted Donettes, those miniature donuts in a bag, and some of the relatives were feeding them to him one after the other.

On Christmas morning, we did not have presents to open. There was no way to bring the gifts with us. The vacation was the gift. Learning to swim outside in the warm sun in December was exhilarating and fun. We had a good dinner on Christmas Eve and then again on Christmas day. One time we ate chicken wings from Hooters. My cousin Kyle showed me how to eat a chicken wing, or at least in one bite. He had a technique. But I ate them normally. In the morning, my grandfather scratched my back. My parents liked that. "Getting the back scratched!"

Then, the rest of the trip mostly evolved around the pool, the weather, the condo, and spending time with family.

When we got back to the house, there was at least a foot of snow on the driveway. My father parked on the street. Had our neighbors been home, the driveway might have been snow-blowed, but they had also gone on vacation and were away.

    My father had to climb over a mound of snow at the beginning of the driveway, made by the snowplow from all the snow on the street, then go through the snow up the driveway and into the garage. He started his snowblower and as we waited in the car he cleared the driveway. Then my mother drove into the garage. I went inside. I looked out the window and saw my father pushing his snowblower down to the street. He shoveled the walkway and deck too.

Chapter 6

Through winter, I stayed inside and played with my toys in the basement. My toy truck amused me. Building towers with miniature toy blocks did too. I continued to play with those the most through spring and then into summer. The basement sort of became my little area, just as the small patch of woods beside the house was upon the changing seasons, the grass growing, dandelions, the sun, then drifting seeds into the wind. I often found salamanders, built forts, and climbed trees in the patch of woods. I was in awe of the woods at night, scared from the scary movies that I had watched, and amazed by the silhouette of trees under the light of the moon and the shadows they cast into the yard. But under the sun, I was playful and frolicked from game to game and project to project.

I built forts with fallen branches. I collected all that I could find and then leaned the branches against a tree around the circumference of its trunk. There were a few logs that had sunken partially into the earth. Half the log lay above the ground and the other half lay below. They rolled out easily, but sometimes after a rainstorm they were waterlogged and much heavier than they normally were. Even so I checked to see what was underneath. Now and then I struggled, because of the extra water weight, but after rolling the log out of the ground there was almost always something to catch. There were often at least a few salamanders. They were the only organisms under the logs about which I was excited and curious. I picked them up and carefully held them cupped in my hands. Their adaptations and complexions fascinated me. Deep red stripes ran along their backs, and sometimes one or two had yellow spots on their undersides, their bellies. Finding a salamander with spots was rare. I brought one inside once to show my parents, and they told me to bring the salamander back outside. Then I went back inside because it was getting dark outside. I went into the basement.

I was still full of energy. I opened the container of blocks and dumped the blocks onto the floor. The container was made of tin. Open, its edges were sharp. I left it open anyway and set it aside, then started building a tower. I imagined that I was building a city. One tower was larger than the others. To me, it was my take then of a skyscraper. I designed it. I built it. And then I tripped and fell toward it. I shifted my weight and fell off to the side. My arm hit the tin container first, right on its open edge.

I stood up. I felt all right. But my arm was throbbing. The underside of my wrist had a wound, and then its pink flesh turned red, and there was liquid.

I walked upstairs as some blood dripped down my arm. My parents were in the living room.

"Mom, Dad," I said.

"What is it, Andrew?"

"My arm."

They sprung up from the couch.

"Oh my God, what happened?"

"I fell on my blocks," I said.

"Den, he might need stitches."

My father got on the phone. I held my arm upright.

"It's all right," said my mother. "Hang in there."

In minutes I was in an ambulance with my mother, and my father followed us to the hospital in his car. We went into a room. I sat on the table. The doctor arrived. He talked with my parents and then began sealing the gash with dissolvable stitches.

"There, all done." He wrapped my arm in bandages.

"Thank you," I said.

"Thank you!" said my mother.

We stopped for ice cream on the way home. Stopping for ice cream was usually a treat. My father ordered grape nut ice cream and so did I. Then we went back to the house. I waited for my arm to heal. And that took over a week. But the next day I was back outside and in the basement, playing, designing spaces, making forts or towers, as my mishap flashed back, day turned to night, silhouettes spread across the sky and shadows cast down in the moonlight.

Chapter 7

All of my maternal relatives were in town for the week. Some of them I hardly saw except around the holidays and periodically in the summer. My aunt Linda lived in Maryland, and my uncle Tony lived in Florida and Ohio between successions of commercial flights. He was a pilot, and he traveled often. They were all in town for the big day at the end of the week. My aunt Linda was getting married, and her wedding was being held in town where she grew up. In the meantime, we all went to the beach. We met everyone at my grandparents' house. They were waiting outside, looking at my grandfather's old Volkswagen Beetle.

I jumped out of the car. "Uncle Tony!" I said.

"Hey dude. You've gotten a bit bigger since the last time I saw you."

I started high-fiving him.

"Let's go, let's go."

"Are you going to go on some rides today?"

"Yes!"

"Well I'm ready. We're just waiting on your mom."

She had gone inside. I was a bit impatient. I wanted to drive to the beach with my aunt Gina. The last time that I had ridden with her she did donuts in a parking lot. I thought that it was as exciting as some of the rides at the beach. The amusement park sat right next to the beach. Some parts were even connected. There was a pier with restaurants, bars, and shops. All around were pizza joints and pier fries. I had not eaten lunch. I liked the pier fries. They're French fries made at the pier, and to me they were a treat at that beach. My mother came outside. We all packed into two cars and drove to the beach.

First my relatives ordered pizza by the slice, then I ordered pier fries. We ate on benches by a fountain and statues as seagulls soared overhead and some waddled along the pavement. Afterward, we bought some tickets for rides.

I went through the funhouse with my uncle many times. There were red and blue and green and yellow bean bags hanging from the ceiling, and as I walked between them, they knocked me around. Painted on one wall was a genie and perhaps on another were stars and a saint. On the ground was a hypnotic circle, one that slowly spun in a continuous motion. I never got tired of it. But I was urged to go on other rides. We rode the bumper cars, the log flume, the teacups, the pirate ship, the roller coaster, and more. By the time we ran out of tickets, I was exhausted, yet ready for more. We spent the rest of the afternoon on the beach, walking on the wet sand or sitting in the sun. It was the first time that I had heard another language. I asked, "What is that?"

"C'est français," said my mother.

I listened to the ocean, that is, Océane. The combination of the two excited me. Then, after a while, I overheard my mother tell her sister about my accident with the toy blocks, the gash and stitches on my arm. "He was tough," she said.

"Let me see it," said my aunt Gina.

I showed her the scar. It had healed in the shape of an arch.

"Wow, look at that," she said. Then to my mother, "All the girls will think he's tough."

My mother smiled. "Yes he is."

We left the beach before sunset. Three days later, it was the big day. I wore a fitted little suit. They wanted me to look nice at the event. My brother and I were the ring bearers. I thought that bringing the ring down the aisle and giving it to the bride, Linda, will be fun. I was excited. The ceremony was held at the Cathedral of the Immaculate Conception. We had to wait outside for a while. There were many groups of people talking on the grass, mostly either distant relatives or longtime friends of my grandfather. Perhaps some were his shipmates and their families. There was hardly anyone else under five years old. I watched two girls dressed in white doing cartwheels in the sun. They were older than I was. I tried a cartwheel and did half a rotation before landing upright. "That's enough," said my mother. "You're going to get your nice clothes dirty."

Then the church bells rang. Everyone rushed inside at once and jammed the front entrance. I made it inside and sat down beside my family. We were all seated toward the back. The inside of the church had a floral scent. There were white ceilings arched high and pillars and archways all around. The windows had stained glass of various shapes and patterns and arched with the walls. Art, I thought—refracting light through consciousness.

Before long I was walking down the aisle. There was no flower girl. I wondered, where are the girls from outside, doing cartwheels? I was a bit nervous. I held the small pillow in one hand, with the ring sitting on top, and with my other hand I held down the skin above my cheeks to ease my dimples then. I walked down the aisle and thought I heard my grandfather laughing. There was his deep Italian laugh. Then there was more. And then my brother nudged me. I smiled and approached the altar. Linda was smiling, waiting for her ring to be delivered.

Then she and her fiancé received their rings. And they got married. After that we went to the reception. Food was served, the cake cut, champagne poured, and I danced with the girls that were doing cartwheels outside earlier.

After a while my mother said, "Time to go."

"No!" I said.

"It's past your bedtime, mister."

"No."

In any case, I walked with her to the car. I slept soundly on the drive back to the house. I went up to my bedroom and got into bed. It was a good day.

Chapter 8

By that time Nico had a group of friends from school that he hung out or played sports with. He was three years older than I was, quieter, and more introverted. Most of his friends were outgoing and adventurous. Some of them liked to skateboard. My brother usually did not skateboard, but because his friends were often skateboarding at the house, I wanted to try the sport. Anthony was his best friend, and he got me into skateboarding. I had to use his skateboard at first before getting my own. We had a few small ramps placed on the driveway that I rode up, then rode down. I did little on a skateboard other than ride around at that point, but I practiced often. I wanted to be as good as the others were. They knew how to ollie, nollie, kickflip, heelflip, manual, all the fundamental tricks that were extreme and exciting to me. I studied their techniques, I formed my own, and they never stopped evolving, adapting more styles, and learning more tricks. I continued practicing, was almost always playing sports, doing activities, or exploring trails and wooded areas.

Not all of my brother's friends practiced action sports. He had met someone in class, Nestor, who enjoyed playing soccer and had a younger brother a year older than I was. Their mother and my mother were friends. Sometimes they talked on the phone for hours. When we all got together, they talked and chatted as the rest of us played or passed the time.

We all often went to the beach or a nearby lake, or else we went to an amusement park, a water park, and sometimes both. I liked that. Other times we went to their house, or they came to ours. Nestor's younger brother Weston liked to watch movies, and so did I. We watched movies at the house, and most frequently we must have watched *Austin Powers* and after that *Mean Girls*. We watched the movies all the way through, multiple times even, in one sitting. We only paused the movie if we heard the ice cream truck. This was an exciting moment, hearing the ice cream truck—and how those treats complemented the movie. Throughout the film, I thought of myself as Austin Powers. Just, different. Especially during *Mean Girls*. He was an endearing character. I said his phrase, "Yeah baby yeah!" and some others from the movie, thinking of the mojo he usually had.

Another movie that came out around that time was *Home Alone*. That was a modern Christmas movie classic to me. I made some booby traps with string outside and around the house. I enjoyed being creative, practicing art, and in a way that involved creativity. I admired the main character in *Home Alone*, Kevin. Whenever my parents got tangled up in some string around the house, they yelled, "Andrew!" the same way McCallister yelled, "Kevin!"

Other than my preschool buddies, I mostly hung out with my brother's friends and Weston, or I played on the driveway or in the yard. Then my neighbors at the end of the street moved and another family moved in from California, but they had also lived in Massachusetts.

One evening as I was making some sort of structure from string in the house, the new neighbors came over and introduced themselves. I had tied a piece of string across the foyer doorway and thought of making a kind of woven archway. I went into the dining room. They came inside. Mrs. R walked into the room and tripped. "Oh my God," said my mother. "I'm so sorry."

My father yelled my name, and they laughed. I walked into the room.

"It's okay," she said.

"He does these things all around the house. Dennis and I tell him to draw them on paper."

She put her arm around her son. "This is Louis."

"Hello," I said.

"Why don't you boys go and get to know each other, play outside."

We walked off. I showed Louis the basement, then my patch of woods outside. He also enjoyed the outdoors, especially nature, as though it is a language and an art of God and the universe.

Louis and I explored the woods as the sun went down. He told me about where he had lived, and California interested me, its beauty, its coasts, mountains, and clear skies. When he mentioned Massachusetts, I thought of the Boston Red Sox and going to a game. I got excited to play baseball.

His family had traveled to Europe many times; they had just gotten back from France, I believe, and that's when they moved in. Louis told me about his time in Paris. The best part, he thought, were the crepes.

"Do you like pancakes?" he asked.

"Yes."

"Crepes are better."

"Okay. I'll ask my dad to make some."

Paris seemed serene. Louis went by Gwynn. I thought of the Eiffel Tower, and I must have pictured the Louvre, the cobblestone streets, and the Seine. I even imagined eating a crepe, having a cup of decaf coffee, and another with a mademoiselle. Then Gwynn's mother called for him. It was time to go inside. We were having a block party at the end of the week, and I asked if he wanted to go to it. They were all already planning on going. Yes! I thought. Excited, I had dinner, and then I worked on the doorway adornment afterward.

Chapter 9

There was a cul-de-sac at the end of the street. In the middle was an island of land. We lived just before it on the street. During the summer my father sometimes mowed the grass on the island. It was a good spot for a block party. The adults set up the grills and chairs and tables. Some of the kids went to my neighbor's pool and waited for the block party to start. Since I had learned to swim in Florida, I liked pools, lakes, and the ocean even more. Instead we came up with games to play at the block party, mostly on the island of land or around it on the street, just as we had done on my other neighbor's trampoline before going to the pool. There were the beach games, wiffle ball, kickball, football and soccer. For the party we decided on having a bike race. And from the trampoline, we had raced down the street and around the cul-de-sac in snow pants and jackets, running, sweating, then undressed and jumped in the pool. I thought that I swam smoothly, that the water felt soft and crisp. In the lake, it got warm on the surface, then the water gradually cooled swimming toward the bottom, a little way out from the beach. At the ocean, the water often felt cool and refreshing, and I swam in the waves all afternoon. I had laid on my towel with the sun overhead.

Everyone decided on biking after dinner. We went from the pool to the trampoline for new games. Gwynn and I were flashed and mooned by my neighbor's friends. It was a thrill. I thought of Austin Powers. We jumped on the trampoline ecstatically. We did flips and spins. We had a lot of energy. My brother was already at the block party.

All the excitement worked up our appetites. Everyone on the street brought food. The fathers worked the grills. Tables were spread with boxes of pizza, salads, casseroles, coleslaw, chips, salsa, bread, butter, pickles, drinks, desserts. Gwynn and I filled our plates with food. We formed a circle on the grass with the other kids and ate. The trampoline absorbed me. The pearl white moon. And the flash of light. I ate in reverie the entire time.

Gwynn's sister was about five years older than we were. My neighbor must have known that I liked *Austin Powers*. After dinner, she got me to say one of my favorite lines in all the movies. "Okay," I said. "Mary, you are a sexy beast."

"Aw, thank you."

I went and hid in the woods. I listened to the birds. Some flew overhead. I watched them. I stayed there until it was time for the bike race.

We all lined up on the road. Five of us on bikes. We were supposed to ride around the cul-de-sac ten times and whoever finished first won. The prize was a pack of sparklers. I wanted to win the bike race. July 4 was coming up, and I not only enjoyed sparklers on holidays, at festivities and events, but I also liked to bike. Then someone blew a whistle.

I took off. I pumped my legs fast. Gwynn and I were up front. We must have been some of the older kids in that group. We all rode around the circle again and again on kids' bikes, and sitting on a big rock in the island of land in the middle of the circle were the older girls, my neighbor and her friends. I experienced the flash and recalled the moon. Excited, I rode on. A big toy truck appeared in the street. I went around it. There was a gully. I flipped over the handlebars, landed on the grass. I lay on the ground for a moment, then I got up. My neighbor and her friends rushed over. "Are you okay?"

My boy smiled. "Yeah, baby, yeah," I said.

Chapter 10

In Kindergarten, my school day started at 12:00 p.m. The bus drove down the street and picked me up in front of the house. The older kids had to walk to the end of the street to catch the bus. I liked having the extra time in the morning. I sat on the couch or at the counter, sometimes with decaf coffee and a bit of cream. My brother had to catch the bus at 8:00 a.m., and since we shared a bedroom, I got out of bed at the same time he did. When he and the other kids walked up the street, although I had four more hours until the bus came for me, sometimes I went with them. I either rode my scooter or skateboard. On occasion, if I took the scooter, I carried someone else's backpack. Gwynn also took the early bus; the first graders had a full day.

If the weather was nice, for the rest of the morning I played outside. I had many hobbies. Since school had started, there were extracurricular activities and study materials. Memorization came part of my nightly routine. States and their capitols had to be learned, and various geographies, bodies of water, geometries too. Basic mathematics had to be practiced. I went around my patch of woods or rode my skateboard up and down the driveway trying to study a bit more before catching the bus, after having gone over my worksheets the night before.

I recalled the first day of kindergarten being slightly nerve-wracking, and then I was full of excitement going to school. I hung out with the boys, and I was good to the girls. I thought that some of them were cute. I had a crush on Gina. She was Italian. I thought of my grandparents, Nana and Papa, and I wondered if maybe hers were also from Italy. My friend Gabriel liked baseball. I went over to his house before school one day and we played catch on his driveway. I also played catch with my friend Joe but with a football in his yard. Then we found a star in the woods. It was made of plastic, and we both thought that it had fallen from the sky. When we left for school, we brought the star with us to show our class. Other kids brought puzzles or drawings, books, crafts, a hamster once. Another friend, Ben, was into math, but in class we mostly made towers with blocks or puzzles with the numbered blocks. I invited him over to my house before school.

Playdates were only a few hours long, and they were always in the morning before school. Arrive at 9:00 a.m., play outside for a couple hours, eat lunch, then ride the bus to school. Ben came over and I showed him my skateboard. I set up a ramp in the middle of the driveway. He got on a scooter, and I got on my skateboard. We rode down the driveway, gained speed, went up the ramp and down the other side, then rode up the driveway and went again. We never got tired of it. I said, "Check this out, Ben."

I tried an ollie. I jumped in the air, the skateboard stayed on the ground. One foot landed on the tail end of the board and the other end flung up at my mouth.

"Careful," Ben said.

"Mhm."

"You all good?"

I nodded. I tasted metal and felt around my gums. I remembered eating hot food, feeling the roof of my mouth. Ben and I rode on. When we ate lunch, grilled cheese sandwiches, I dipped my sandwich in ketchup and that stung my mouth. Ben and I finished lunch. And then we went outside and waited for the school bus.

Another time that year, I went to Ben's house before school. We explored the woods behind his house. We went through a wet area past the edge of his yard. Then we came out at a stream. We jumped over the water twice. First to see the other side. And then again to get back to his house.

Ben's basement was carpeted, painted, and finished. There was a big tv. He had a PlayStation. Right away I thought that his basement was great, a nice open space with sunlight beginning to stream in late that morning. We played a skateboarding game on his PlayStation. His mother asked if we wanted haircuts, and both of us did. She was awesome. Ben went and got his haircut first and

I continued playing the video game. Ten minutes later he came down and looked dapper. Then I went up.

"How do you want your hair cut?" Ben's mother asked.

"Like Ben's," I said.

She cut my hair fast, styled and even gelled it like Ben's after his haircut, lifting the front a bit and combing off to the side. After lunch we rode his bus to school.

Our teacher went by Ms. Bougie. She was a young woman. I liked her last name. During breaktime, Ms. Bougie said, "I like your haircut, Andrew."

"Thank you, Ms. Boobie."

"Wait." I was flustered.

"Anything else?"

"I like your shirt, Ms. Bougie."

"Thanks Andrew."

My cheeks uplifted.

I went to play with Ben and Joe. That day we built towers with blocks. Other days we played card games, board games, with Legos, made drawings, did worksheets.

We made the towers on the floor in the cubby area off to the side of the classroom. That was our usual spot to build with blocks or Legos if we weren't sitting at a table drawing. Gina went into the bathroom, and at that same time, a boy with special needs walked into the room with his helper. "Everyone, this is Ned. Say hello, Ned." He smiled and clapped his hands enthusiastically, while making peculiar noises. He looked around the room dreamily, joyously. It must have been exciting, a world totally new to him. It was his first time in the classroom, and he collected items from a box next to the paper bin. He walked over to the box clapping his hands, then lifted his shirt and clapped his belly. It delighted Ned. He rushed over to us in the cubby area and checked out our block towers. Then the bathroom door opened. Gina walked out. I got up and went into the bathroom and sat on the toilet seat. It was warm. I liked it, and kindergarten. The excitement continued as Ned went down the hall. Breaktime finished after that. We all sat cris-crossed in a circle on the carpeted area, winding down from the school day, waiting for the buses.

Chapter 11

The next schoolyear started, after kindergarten transitioned into summer, and I was in the first grade. Teachers assigned more homework, and we went to school from 8:00 a.m. to 3:00 p.m., played organized sports after school, and had tests and quizzes in school. Over the summer, the only schoolwork that had been assigned was to keep a reading log. The teacher asked us to read every day, and I did most days. I tried writing my own book. I read the first page of a book and attempted to write the first page of my book. I got down only a line or two, then stopped. I read some young adult books all the way through, and I expected myself to write my own all the way through. The introduction could have been about creating a form of art through literature, the style within, in the moment then, and in the moment while writing it.

In the first grade, I became fond of playing sports. There was baseball, skiing, football, and soccer. I played on a team in every sport except for skiing. During winter, my family went to a ski resort for the weekend. We stayed at a bed and breakfast, and in the morning we went out to the slopes. I was nervous at first, the skis were rentals, I had to acclimate to the balance on skis. My parents and my brother rode up the magic carpet with me and then slowly skied down the bunny slopes as I learned how to turn, stop, and balance. At first, my technique was the "pizza." Every turn that I made my ski tips pointed inward as the tails slid apart, wide at the end, altogether shaped triangularly almost like a slice of pizza. Many novice skiers had the same form. It was a way to slow down while still moving forward, but it's a bad habit for the skier and rough on the trail, sort of plowing as opposed to gliding atop the snow. However, I quickly learned to turn with my skis parallel. Then I rode on the chairlift. I went down the mountain. I even raced someone on one of the trails beside the chairlift. I went down the blue squares, the intermediate trails. The snow softened substantially by the afternoon. We stopped skiing when the sun began to set over the distant mountains. I was still stimulated when the day ended, refreshed from the exercise, thrilled for the next day. What an awesome first time skiing, I thought.

Then spring came and I started playing baseball. I was in a division of Little League called the Minor League. Most schools offered it starting in first grade, and most boys played. I had already practiced often in the front yard with my father or by myself. In Minor League, the coaches, who were also fathers, pitched to us underhand. I was already used to my father pitching. He threw overhand to me in the front yard. I hit home runs often—fly balls past the edge of the yard and into the patch of woods. I had practiced for school baseball a lot, and I did well in the Minor League.

My brother Nico also played baseball. He was not as enthusiastic about the sport as I was. One time we were practicing our swing in the basement. We set up a tee in an open area, then hit a tennis ball against the wall and took turns at the tee. I studied his form. I was a scientist, as I enjoyed the sciences in school. But one time, as I watched his back foot pivot, the bat came around and hit my cheekbone hard. It hurt, and I was silent for a moment, then yelled as I ran upstairs. It bruised for a little while. The kids at school were interested and got more into sports. "You were playing baseball inside?"

"With a tennis ball," I said.

Football had started in August, just before the schoolyear had begun. Joe and I lined up next to each other. Our school and another district combined for first grade football and had three different teams. Soccer had several teams, and they were all players from our school district. I played soccer in the first grade.

Our team colors were lime-green, and we were called the Chili Peppers. We all ran around the field full of energy. I enjoyed playing soccer most when I either scored a goal or played goalie and stopped a goal. Ben was on the Red Foxes and carried his team. We were the lime-green Chili Peppers, and we were good.

The Red Foxes and the Chili Peppers played each other once or twice. The time that I played goalie we won. Toward the end of the game, Ben dribbled past our whole team and approached the goal. He kicked the soccer ball, I caught it. My heart raced. I then punted the soccer ball downfield. Gabriel scored the winning goal. After the game, both teams lined up and shook hands, and then we all had snacks.

Our school day was split into several blocks and during each block we learned a different subject. Math came naturally, and English and language arts did too, but during math I may have been more attuned, even working ahead on the word problems and the tables. Art class was my favorite block of the school day. I created all kinds of art, on canvas and on paper, with pencils and paints, objects and displays with clay, string, beads, yarn. I painted or drew at the beginning of every block. I drew abstract designs. I showed a drawing to my classmate Dana one day. It was full of complex shapes in one big abstract design. The entire page was covered with connected lines that formed shapes, but nothing was filled in. She said, "Color it, Andrew. That will be fun."

"Okay Dana."

That night I colored my drawing and in the morning I showed her. "I colored it for you," I said.

"I like it," she said. She gave me a hug.

At recess, I either played games with the girls by the shrubs or played on the playground or played kickball on the softball field. Another classmate and I sometimes watched Ned on the swings as he ran around the playground. It seemed like he had developed his own kind of language. It sounded unusual, and I found it interesting.

"Goocha gadagadagadagada," Ned sometimes said.

And then some other kids around the playground went, "Gada gadagadagadagada."

He may have been saying hello and good morning to nice day, having an exciting time outside.

Ned rode my bus along with all the other neighborhood kids. We sat in the back and Ned sat up front. There were no assigned seats, but Ned always sat in the same seat, one row behind the bus driver on the right side. Our bus picked us up at the school last.

We waited on the softball field for it to arrive. Sometimes we played catch or frisbee or else sat on the benches.

"How many baby teeth do you have left?"

"None."

"Same."

"Look at the peach fuzz on my face."

"Yeah."

"Are you getting body hair?"

"No, not yet."

The bus arrived and we got on. Everyone walked down the aisle and sit in their usual seats. Ned was the only kid in the front row. And then there was a commotion. We heard from the kids up front: Ned had his penis out and he was shifting it around with his hand. The bus driver looked up in the mirror, then turned around. "Ned, put that away!" He then had a tantrum, and he bawled for most of the bus ride to his house.

I played kickball after lunch when we went outside for recess. There were two captains that rotated day to day, and they each picked teams one by one. Anyone could play, and because players were drafted alternately, the teams were almost always even. I kicked the ball and fielded the ball well. Not everyone was good, it was first-grade recess, but some players took the games seriously, and they were fast, the innings flipped in moments, the recesses lasted half an hour. Miles, Mark, and I were the top three picks for our team. They were both athletic. They thought I was a beast. We stood against the fence as our team captain finished drafting players. Mark pulled out a piece of paper. "Check this out," he said.

On the page were several images of bikini models. They posed elegantly. Each model had a unique complexion, a luster, a relaxed emotion. All of them seemed like nice women.

"Yes!"

"Amazing, Mark."

He held the piece of paper with both hands. We admired it. Then the rest of our team came over to the fence.

"Let me see that," said Tim. He folded it and put it in his pocket.

Our captain had the last pick, and it was Taylor. He had little coordination on the field. When he was up to bat at home plate, the players on the other team moved in a bit. And when the inning switched or ended, he went out to the outfield.

The game started and the matchup was even. It went back and forth throughout the entire recess. One team scored one inning, and the other team scored the next. Miles pitched for our team that game. He wound up and rolled the ball toward home plate. Sometimes the pitchers added spin to their roll, and the ball curved along its path toward home plate. Mark and I and two other kids were in the infield. We fielded every groundball, blooper, and some flyballs that went into the outfield. Taylor stood off toward rightfield lackadaisically, picking dandelions as some kids called it in Little League. The next inning there were two outs. It was the last inning. Taylor was up to bat at home plate, and after that, if he kicked the ball well, it was going to be the top of the order again.

The pitcher rolled the ball. Taylor kicked and basically missed it. The ball dribbled slowly back to the pitcher. He fielded it and then threw the ball to the first baseman, and Taylor was out. Recess ended.

Miles, Mark, and I were going to be up next, respectively. We could have scored and won the game. We wanted another at-bat. We kicked long fly balls or line drives. Miles and Mark were upset. They ran after Taylor. He tripped and fell over. The whistles blew. We all went and lined up at the back door.

Chapter 12

Summer and our time off from school seemed to go by fast. We made the most out of the time that we had. I could not get enough of the light nights, longer days, the dog days of summer. On the last day of school I stood on my porch in the sun and thought, soon it'll be the last day of summer vacation and school will start tomorrow. The time in between could have lasted forever. I saw my relatives and was often with friends. We went to all kinds of places, beaches, lakes, mountains, amusement parks. I practiced sports on the days to myself. I liked to skateboard. I played basketball, and I started to play baseball, practicing my swing, with a ball attached to a rope that coiled around the basketball pole and then uncoiled and swooped around as though it was the next pitch. It happened in a perpetual motion, the windup, the pitch and then swing. Over the winter I had brought my skateboard inside and learned how to ollie in the basement. Then, during summer, I tried to learn and ultimately land flip tricks. I brought my skateboard to my grandparents' house, my father's parents, when we all went to see them.

They had a small driveway. With two cars parked, there was little space to practice. I was worried about scratching my father's car. It may have happened once before then, but he thought, once again. "What's this?" he said, examining a small mark on the paint. "It's a scratch!"

I never rode my bike out of the garage after that, or my skateboard and scooter, if the cars were parked inside. When they were not, and if it was a rainy day, I brought some ramps in and practiced inside. Worried about the car, I got my skateboard and went down into my grandparent's basement. My grandfather was on the computer. He looked very calm, very peaceful. I set down my skateboard. "Hi Pepa."

"Hi Andrew. I heard someone coming downstairs. How are you?"

"Good."

"You brought your skateboard."

"Yes." I showed him the underside. "It's an Element."

"Very nice," he said. "Hold on, I'll go upstairs. You be careful skateboarding."

"Okay."

There was also little space to practice skateboarding in their basement but just enough to try and do some tricks. I warmed up with an ollie, then did a few more, then my brother came downstairs with his camera. He wanted to take pictures, so I tried a kickflip. At that time, I always landed with only one foot on the skateboard. He took pictures of me in the air. They came out well. The one in the picture landed smoothly. I tried again and popped up from the tail harder, then again, and again, then *thud*. My skateboard landed on the floor. I felt something hard as a rock in my mouth. I pulled out my tooth, then noticed a small gouge on the tip of my skateboard. I thought of my father's car, then of my tooth. I had already lost all my baby teeth. I began to worry. My brother could tell. "Are you all right?" he asked.

"I think so." I smiled.

He rushed upstairs and said, "Andrew knocked out his tooth!"

"What!"

"No!" I said to myself. My tooth had chipped, and I felt where it had a bit above the gum. It ached: a sensitive, almost electric kind of tooth ache.

"Andrew!"

I went upstairs. They were in the foyer. "My tooth is just chipped," Then smiling, "See?"

My father was relaxed. But my mother was worked up. "I knew you were going to get hurt on that skateboard," she said. "Come here." She hugged me.

"Well…" She looked at it, and then she lightened up and smiled to herself. "We need to get your tooth fixed. Your cousins are coming up next week."

"Yes," I said. In fact, I had been waiting all year to see them the following week.

My mother called the dentist. I went and looked at my tooth in the bathroom. "It happened on his skateboard. Yes, you can fit him in this afternoon? Great, thank you. See you soon." She got off the phone. We drove back to the house shortly after that, and from there I went to see the dentist. My tooth was fixed with bonding, and the ache from the tooth's exposed nerve subsided.

I returned to playing sports the following day, though more carefully than I had been before. My cousins had already been on summer vacation for a month. They had all grown since the last time I saw them. My uncle drove two days straight to the house. He had a big SUV with XM radio. Our cars were modest. Halfway through their trip they stopped and spent the night at my aunt Brenda and uncle Scott's house, and they drove to our house too.

My father's parents owned a cottage by the ocean. The yard was big. It went up into a field, an area with long grass and some weeds, a big space to play baseball. Where the yard transitioned into the fielded area with tall grass marked the homerun. They also had a picnic table behind the cottage where we ate lunch, fresh seafood, clams and lobster. Across the street was a house that my relatives had rented and stayed in for the week. My uncle brought fireworks. We set them off just after dark by the ocean. I had the greatest time lighting the fuse and then running back and watching the show. The kids took walks along the beach and searched the rocks covered in seaweed for crabs. We picked them up and they pinched our fingers with their little claws. Then we put them back on the rock where we had found them. It delighted me. There were some large rocks without seaweed too. I thought of those as baseball gloves, in a way, catcher's mitts or first baseman's gloves. I practiced pitching by throwing small rocks toward the middle of large ones, even sidearm by skimming flat rocks across the surface of the water. I was trying to be the greatest baseball player that I could be, and I thought of it almost as an artform.

My parents, brother, and I lived less than an hour away. We spent the night at the house and drove to the cottage in the morning. Other times that week, everyone came to the house. My father worked the grill, and I showed my cousins around the house, the yard, the wooded areas. Then we went to an amusement park nearby and connected to its entrance was a water park. The latter had all kinds of pools and slides. The best attraction was in the center of the park, I thought, waiting for the big pirate head to dump water on us from twenty feet above, as water sprayed and splashed all around. I went there often with my brother and friends, mostly Nestor and Weston. Our mothers both worked at schools then and had the summers off. They sat in chairs as we bounced around the water park. With my cousins, we only went to the amusement park. We rode maybe every ride, and we went on a couple of rides again and again. One was a roller coaster, and another was inside a big yellow dome. We exited the dome and then got back in line at the entrance. Inside we sat in carts and spun around an axis and whirled in circles that spun around another axis. A kaleidoscopic light show displayed on the walls and an instrumental orchestra played from the speakers. That went on all afternoon. Throughout the morning, it had been that with the roller coaster. The next day was July 4.

That night I asked my parents, "What time are we going to the cottage?"

"Actually, tomorrow we're going to a different cottage. Your father's friend invited us to his. It's at the lake!"

Awesome, I thought.

"There will be other kids too."

"What about Kyle and Kelsey and Matt?"

"They're going to your grandparent's cottage. You'll see them again before they drive back to their house."

"Okay."

It was my first time at the cottage and at that lake. Anxious and excited to go swimming, the scenery passed in reverie looking out the window from the back seat. We drove down a dirt road that winded at times and went on a long way into the woods, the air flowing through the windows and fresh lake water and pine scents too. Then we parked and walked down a staircase made of rock. They had a rustic cottage by the lake, pine trees all around, a small sandy beach, and a metal dock, to which a boat was tied, and it shone in the sun and the water sparkled and rippled along its path to the shore. We were greeted by everyone, several families, there must have been around twenty people at the cottage. Some were familiar, but I met many of them for the first time. "Say hello, Shawn."

"Hello."

"Hello," I said.

"Shawn, take Andrew to see the other kids."

We went across the yard from which big pine trees stretched high and wide and their roots bulged from the ground and we sat at a picnic table off to the side by the beach. "This is my sister Leanne," said Shawn. "That's Christian and Alex, they're brothers."

Christian and I rode the same bus and lived one street apart. We recalled Ned on the bus, and we laughed.

"What grade are you going into?" Julianne asked.

"Second," I said.

"I'm going into third, so is Christian."

"I'm going into first," said Alex.

"Me too," said Shawn.

I looked around at the lakeside setting, the placid water, clear sky and sun. The sound of the water gently washing up, quietly pulling away with the breeze. The trees, the smell, the small island directly ahead of the beach. Sitting on a chair by the firepit, I noticed someone else who rode my bus. She sat poised, as calm as the setting. It was Tessa. I thought of the moon glowing in the sun.

Moments later we were on the boat going tubing. What a thrill! I gripped the handles as tight as possible. I was afraid of falling off the tube and floating in the open water. But one time when we were going through a heavy swell, I let go at the top of a wave and launched into the air. I flew for at least a second, two, or three, it seemed like. Then I landed in the water. I watched the boat drive on. I spun around one way, then the other. I looked down. My legs tread calmly in the sunlight underwater, darkness all around. I swam vigorously toward the boat as it turned around and came my way slowly and then stopped before me. I climbed aboard, sat down. The sun felt so warm, the breeze refreshing. Wrapped in my towel, I sat on the back seat and watched the others go tubing.

We then moored the boat to a small island. There were other boats and people in the water and on the island. A few of them climbed a tree and stood atop a boarded platform. Someone from the ground handed them a long rope. Then they swung down and went out over the water and then let go and plunged into the water. An older boy did a flip in the air. He entered the water perfectly and made no splash. Everyone watching cheered. When it was my turn, I spun around once in the air before going feet first into the water, and then I swam back to the boat. I fully dried off then and wrapped myself in a towel.

After swimming all day, we sat in chairs on the beach and watched the fireworks around the lake. There were colorful displays of light in every direction, across the lake, down the cove, on either side, and right beside us. Above the lake was a window to the universe, the moon still, unmoving, a few stars arching. Its light cast a path along the water before me. Mesmerized, I thought of the moon.

We drove to my grandparents' cottage and saw my relatives there before the week ended. Many days passed. Gwynn and I explored the woods around the neighborhood. We followed a trail to a pond and caught frogs. We called it the frog pond. It was also home to a big turtle, a legendary creature to us, who lay in the shallow, murky waters along the edge of the pond or on branches poking out above the water's surface. It came to the water's edge while we were there. We caught a frog and let it go beside the turtle, then very swiftly, the turtle lurched its head and nudged the frog. The next moment, it was gone, leaving a cloud of silt in the water where it had been perched, and the frog lay still, resting on its rearend and hind legs. Then we went back to Gwynn's house and climbed trees. His cats watched from the yard. They also climbed trees. Or they hunted mice. Outside they were always on the prowl, Shadow and Lola. I dropped down from the bottom branch and Lola came up to me. She rubbed her head against my leg. I thought that it was incredible. I petted her back. Then Gwynn came down from the tree. We went inside. Later he invited me to his family's lake house. I was excited and eager to go up there.

We went the following week. We left in the morning and drove all day and along the way we passed bodies of water and small towns and mountains. When we reached a high enough altitude, my ears popped. The road at one point became unpaved. We rattled along the dirt road for a while, and the road kept going.

We settled in at the lake house. Gwynn showed me upstairs. We set our bags down and went outside for the rest of the day. The lake was completely still, almost like a big sheet of tinted glass. There was the sound of the outdoors, the trees in the light wind, and the moment the sun went down, the calls of the loons resonated from the reflective water, the exquisite, dreamy sounds echoing under the moon. And then they began again, stronger and perkier, at sunrise.

There were not any large motorboats on the lake. And perhaps the loons mostly rested from around sunrise to sunset. So naturally, the lake was quiet throughout the day. It was tranquil, deep in the wilderness. Gwynn and I rode kayaks through the morning fog. Later we went for a hike. And then we ended the day at a sandy beach near his lake house. Down the road was a small wooden bridge. Gwynn jumped into the water. "Did you touch the bottom?" I asked.

"Yes. Your turn."

I jumped in. The water was warm. It felt crisp and pure. I swam to the side and climbed up the rocks along the bank. We went again.

"Come on. Let's swim out to the raft."

"Okay."

"On your mark, get set, go!"

We set off in the water and reached the raft together. Gwynn climbed on first, and then I did. We sat on the edge of the dock. He said that he had touched a vagina.

"What did it feel like?"

"Well, just like skin."

Our legs dangled off the raft and into the water. Several minnows swam around. They nibbled at my toes. I smiled.

The next day we ate lunch in town and then drove back to Crystal Lane. I slept in the car for most of the way. I thanked Gwynn and his mother. It was just us that had gone up to the lake. I had an excellent time. And just in time for school to start. Then the last day of summer vacation came and I went out on the deck. I stood in the same spot as I had on the last day of school, the first day of summer vacation, and the sunlight shone golden. I sat down, just a bright boy with a sweet tooth, musing on the schoolyear, sports, the other kids. I went to bed early that night.

Chapter 13

My father had asked if I wanted to play football in the second grade, and I said that I did. I played hard at practices and in games. Thinking of us running up and down a field wearing ten pounds of gear then in a lighthearted and determined manner almost seemed funny, then calling the huddle, following the cadence.

So, I was back on the football field, and I continued playing football through high school. It was a full-contact sport from then on. I tried to be in on every play, and liked making big plays on defense, good tackles, turnovers. My body had some extra bulk in the second grade, my muscles conditioned, my agility developed. I was built in the second grade, an early developer, and a fast runner at that age. I led the sprints with Joe. I wanted to be a running back and to score a touchdown. In the league that I was in, called Pee Wee football, there was a weight limit that you could not exceed to qualify as a running back. Whatever it was—around one-hundred pounds—I weighed maybe ten pounds over the limit. My friend fasted prior to the weigh-in so he would qualify as a running back. They were the skilled players on offense, the running backs, and I was a lineman. They ran with the ball, scored touchdowns, and I blocked the other team's players for them. But I held the ball every play on offense; I was the center. After snapping the ball to the quarterback, an opponent and I stood in one spot or in its vicinity, pushing at each other for either the duration of the play or a significant part of it. A couple of little bulls locking horns. Playing some teams, the kids that I went up against were drenched, their jerseys and pants soaked in sweat and water. We went at each other as the skilled players ran around the outside and scored touchdowns.

Joe was our star running back, and at that time another Joe was our star quarterback. He may have been the best player on our team. If Joe got the ball or the other Joe ran with the ball, there was a good chance that they'd score a touchdown. He sometimes ran from side to side, even backward if there was no path or hole going up the middle. Our coach got worked up over that.

"No running east or west, Joe!"

Then, throwing his clipboard on the ground, "None of that dancing crap! North or south! Find the hole and then go!"

As long as the running backs moved us down the field, eventually we scored a touchdown. I probably celebrated more than anyone else when we scored, except for the parents, because it meant that after the kickoff we were on defense. Joe and I were the middle linebackers on defense. We saw the most action, made the most plays, and along with the other defensive backs and linemen, we did not often let up a touchdown.

I had fun on defense. Joe and I stood five yards behind the line of scrimmage and maybe five feet apart on either side of the football. We eagerly waited for the other team to run a play. They broke the huddle, then approached the line of scrimmage. Their quarterback called the cadence.

"Ready…" he said. "Set… Hut!"

The players in their backfield ran around. The lineman squared off with each other, all jammed up in one big clump. Joe and I scanned the field. The play appeared to be flowing toward my side. It was.

Our coach yelled, "It's a sweep! Tackle him!"

I went at their running back full tilt. He ran toward the outside, then tried cutting up field. We collided, our helmets struck, the sound rang. I heard, "Ah!"

Then, "Fumble! Get it, get on it!"

The ball rolled in the other direction. I scrambled to my feet, dove on the ground. I held the ball to my body, practically cradling it, and then I noticed the other team's goal line. I had recovered the fumble on their two-yard line. I was but two yards away from scoring a touchdown.

The referees blew their whistles. Someone was crying. I stood up and joined my teammates. Everyone took a knee. The other team's running back was on the ground. He had hurt his ankle. Everyone was asked to move off to the sideline. Then a parent went out and put a blanket over his leg. Players and coaches patted my back. We went out on the field. Our quarterback then scored a touchdown. We played deep into autumn. We did most football seasons, ending not long before the mountains up north opened and the ski season started.

I had a group of friends in my second-grade class. We had met at recess before and we sat at the same table. We moved around the classroom a lot, experiencing new methods of learning in an interactive setting. It may have been from playing musical chairs that we sat at different tables and in new seats. At the new table, I often drew in my notebook during the intermissions between lessons. They were undetailed drawings, mostly shapes and patterns, innately taking on the appearance of fractals. I drew whatever geometry came to mind. My notebook was soon filled: some notes in the front that went with the worksheets, the handouts, the class materials, and in the back or even in the margins of pages in the front were shapes, patterns, drawings. My mind was full of ingenuity. I wrote from my heart. I worked in a relaxed but fervent manner. I browsed the bookshelf during silent reading. When we wrote after that block, I did in a stream-of-consciousness style, and it was often narrative with bits of then infant intellect. Our teacher read my writing.

"Interesting book, Andrew. What's the title of it?"
"*The Heat Rises.*"
"Hm, I hadn't heard of that book. Is that one of our books?"
"Not yet."
"I see," she said. "That's even more remarkable."

Language was derived to enhance communication. Not muddle it. It is a part of evolutionary consciousness. Language and intellect have evolved parallel to one another and in unison. Intellect is articulated from language, and the more proficient one is, the more articulate the other can be. What then was consciousness derived from? It is a chicken and egg metaphor, with perhaps a more profound meaning, a magnitude and motion.

I wrote in my journal, then drew in my notebook.

Baseball was still my favorite sport, and it continued to be through high school. I enjoyed just playing the sport. I liked batting practice, pitching in the bullpen, fielding ground balls, catching pop flies, having home run derbies. In second grade, that list might have included chewing gum, having sunflower seeds and sports drinks. But I mainly liked to play ball, just play. I played hard on teams, and alone or practicing with someone else, I competed with myself, my previous pitch, swing, catch, and always my fielding. Practices and games were exciting, usually fun, weather permitted. Less enthusiastic about practice, I either wanted to play badly or I was in the mood for a homerun derby. If a game or a practice had been canceled, some other kids and I may have still played inside. I never skipped either. There was about fifteen minutes before I went to practice after getting home from school. My mother arrived at the house when it was time to go to the field. Coming in the door, she said, "Hello, time to go to practice!"

I was upstairs. She came up. "I'm working in my journal."

"You're going to practice, mister. Plus, we can stop at the movie store after."

"Okay."

So, I went to practice. I played and had fun. Then we went to the movie store. There was a deal on Tuesdays and Thursdays. Rent two movies for the price of one. I still watched *Austin Powers,* but I never rented his movies, I owned the whole series on DVD. Action movies were good. So were adventure movies and comedies. Thrillers and scary movies were stimulating. I had to be in the right mood for a romantic movie, and when I was, they were quite affecting. Lovable movies were exciting. I liked *The Sandlot*, and that came from playing baseball so much. At the movie store I almost always rented the classics.

I picked out a movie. My mother was still browsing the shelves. I went to the counter and looked through all the bins of candy. Laffy Taffy, Skittles, Starburst, Ring Pops were just one part of the movie experience. Going to the store was another. It was a rustic structure at the corner of an intersection. The owner, Lucinda, had purchased it and turned it into a movie store. Inside the carpeted floors creaked and groaned. I picked out two pieces of candy.

My mother said, "Hey, this movie looks good! Look, Andrew."

I went over to my mother. "What is it?"

"Here, you can't see?"

"Yes," I said. "I was seeing if you could see."

She put the movie back. "Don't get smart with me, young man."

We checked out and walked down the ramp and got in her car and drove to the house. I worked at my desk, ate dinner, then watched a movie before bed.

As it turned out, there were many kids who liked movies and a lot of the same ones that I liked too. I learned that on the playground playing kickball. Joe and I waited for our turns at the plate. He was into scary movies too. He invited me over to his house for a sleepover. That weekend I went, and my friend Ryan was there too. They're cousins, and we all played football together. On offense, Ryan and I stood on the line as linemen. I was the center, and he was a tackle. We blocked the other team's players for Joe. At the sleepover, Ryan, Joe, and I wrestled and practiced tackling in his living room. There were cushions and pillows and blankets on the floor. I had a baseball game the next day. We all had a lot of energy. Then, after a while, we decided to take a break from roughhousing and go to the movie store. We walked there. The store was close to Joe's house. Lucinda greeted us, then we each picked out a movie and went to the counter. "Nice picks, boys," said Lucinda. She offered us some candy.

"Thank you."

Outside, Randy said, "Let's watch mine first."

"No, my movie first."

"No, mine!"

"Okay. We'll do a coin toss."

We had some coins to buy candy with. I flicked a quarter in the air. "Call it, Ryan."

"Heads."

It was tails.

Joe got the second coin toss right, and we were sleeping over at his house, so we watched the movie that he picked first. We stayed up most of the night and finished watching all three movies, and then we went to bed. We slept in the living room on all the cushions, pillows, and blankets that we had played on.

In the morning, the three of us wrestled on the floor again. The cushions helped. I thought that it may have been softer than on the football field. It was a free-for-all. I got down behind Ryan. Then Joe pushed him. He toppled over, and his elbow hit me right at the mouth. I felt something, like a small rock, under my tongue. And then I felt a gap between my teeth. I smiled at Ryan.

"Aw man" he said.

"What?" asked Joe.

I held out my hand. It was my tooth, the same tooth that had chipped before.

My parents came to pick me up. I missed my baseball game that afternoon and went to see the dentist. In a way, I was injured and could not have played in the game that day. Plus, I was able to practice lightly in the front yard instead. The following week our schedule was mostly dry, and we had a home run derby on one of the off days.

Chapter 14

My whole family had gone to Virginia during winter break. We stayed at my aunt Brenda and my uncle Scott's house. We celebrated the holidays. And then we went again during summer vacation. My father drove us. We left at 8:00 p.m. and arrived the next morning at 8:00 a.m. There was virtually no traffic. We drove south along the highways and for most of the way past midnight we were one of the only cars on the road. My brother and my mother fell asleep. I stayed up, excited for the upcoming week. My father said, "Get some rest, Andrew. We still have seven hours to go."

In two days, we were going to one of the best amusement parks in America, Busch Gardens. And the next day, Kings Dominion. All year I had become increasingly preoccupied and excited for the vacation, the trips to the amusement parks, all the rides, seeing my relatives, and playing sports with them.

Seven hours later we arrived. Brenda greeted us in the driveway. "How was the drive?" she asked.

"Smooth," said my father.

I went up to her and said, "Hello."

"Hey, you!"

Brenda liked physical fitness, nutrition, wellbeing. She went to the gym often, led classes at the YMCA, rode bikes, ran, boxed, and kickboxed. She did a kind of play where she squared off jabbed at the air in front of me, and with each movement, she said, "Bam, bam bam, bam!"

I squared off. "Bam bam!" And she squared off. "Bam bam bam!"

We laughed, then stopped.

"You must be tired!" she said.

"Yes," I said.

I walked inside and went up to Scott. "Hey uncle Scott!" I said and gave him a big high five. I asked about snacks, and we looked in the kitchen for any that might be delicious. There was organic apricot nectar. I drank a glass, then went upstairs. They had a room above their garage that was a big open space. In the corner sat an inflated air mattress. I lay down and went to sleep.

When I woke up, it was nighttime. There was a lot of noise coming from downstairs. I heard my parents, then Scott, then Brenda, then "Y'all." My cousins and their parents were in the house. I went downstairs. "Ay!" everyone said as I entered the room. Uncle Scott was telling a story. He had been biking the night before, and when he got back to the house, he got out a bottle of wine. He used a corkscrew to pull the cork out of the bottle. It slipped and the tip of the coil pierced his thumb. He thought that it had hit a vein because blood squirted around the kitchen and he yelled and then my aunt Brenda yelled and they went back and forth, and as I wondered if we were going to play basketball in the driveway, she said again, "Scott!"

Kyle and Kelsey were sitting at the counter. I sat on a stool beside them. Kyle was drinking a beer. It was similar to a kind that my father had on occasion, a glass bottle IPA, one that at home I had wanted to try since an earlier Fourth of July. I had a little sip of Kyle's. I liked the taste. I enjoyed the feeling of holding a beer bottle in that moment; I felt older than I was. "That's good," I said, and then Kyle went to the refrigerator and got one for me. He popped off the cap with his lighter. I thought that was neat. I held the bottle—cool in the summer heat.

"Wait," said my brother. "Andrew's having a beer?"

"Shh," I said.

"But…"

"That's all right," said my father. "Do you want one?"

"No thanks," said my brother.

I sat on the stool calmly, a beer in hand, delighted that first night on vacation.

It was my first time at Busch Gardens, and immediately I was in awe. I ran around the pathways of the magical world into which I entered. I watched the rides operate. The roller coasters were unlike anything that I had seen up close. They had double loops, corkscrews, spirals, hundred-foot drops at nearly ninety degrees from the vertical. All the thrill rides had a minimum height requirement of maybe forty-eight inches. I suppose I had reached that sometime in the second grade. The lines were not too long, but there were usually big groups of people walking in just as we were, and I walked with them, in the middle of everyone, as both groups went up to the platform excited. I never stood against the measuring sticks. I must have stood out. Then realized, to stand out is miraculous.

We rode every roller coaster several times. Each one was different, and they were all such thrills. Apollo's Chariot, a prominent roller coaster, was exhilarating. The line went fast, and the thrill lasted well after the ride, looping around from the exit and getting back in line. We went over a pond, then beside a river, over troughs in the track, and through the woods very fast. We rolled around to the station and came to a stop. I got off the ride and went up to my father outside. "Come on the roller coaster, dad."

"Yeah, dad. Come on!"

"Okay, okay. Let's go!"

Scott was even more enthusiastic about going on the rides. His favorite might have been the log flume. But we rode in a boat instead of a log. First we went up a conveyor belt and then entered a Tuscan-style building. It was flooded with water but only on the inside. We floated slowly through the upstairs hallways as though they were canals, and there was fire everywhere on either side of us, up the walls and on the ceilings. Large pillars fell above our heads but never on us or our boat. It was loud. And suspenseful. And then both doors at the egress parted and revealed the sky and we slid rapidly down a chute. Then, at the bottom, we plowed through a shallow pool of water. The splash that our boat made was huge. Water poured on us, then we slowed down and came to a stop. We got off the ride drenched.

One side attraction in the middle of the amusement park preoccupied me greatly after lunch. It was a basketball game, which was fun to play, and I wanted to win the grand prize. A big, purple, stuffed animal dinosaur. I had a decent jump shot playing basketball then, and I scored often, but there were stages to the prizes. When I played the first game, I won a keychain; the second game, a small toy; the third game, a bigger toy, or a Beanie Baby. Each time I played the game and won I had the option to trade my previous prize for a slightly better prize. The purple dinosaur was the best prize, I thought. I played game after game. My parents watched.

"He's pretty good," my father said.

"I liked to play softball," said my mother. "And tennis."

I scored more, and I got on a streak. Then I carried the stuffed dinosaur around the amusement park with me. We all later went out to the car and back to the house. That night, I went to sleep cozy.

We went to Kings Dominion the next day and both amusement parks one more time before we left. One place had a water park and the experience was unique. There were two water parks near my house, and I thought that both were good, but neither compared to the new experience, all the different slides and pools and splashing and floating along the lazy river. We lounged in tubes, carried by a swift current. We had been busy that week. It was good to relax. When my cousins and brother got out of the water, I stayed in. The sun shone, and the river never stopped flowing.

We spent the other days in Virginia at the house. I played sports in the front yard, either by myself or with my uncle Scott. It was normally with my father at the house, playing baseball. With Scott, we played football and basketball too. He played basketball in college. He then had a hoop in his driveway, had gotten it as a Christmas present the year before. He was good at basketball. We played two games, Around the World and Horse. Scott had been a shooting guard playing basketball, and I only had a decent jump shot then. If I won, then we played baseball; if I lost, we still played baseball. In any case, we practiced baseball a lot. The coaches still pitched in the league that I was in, but I began practicing at home with my father, and it was mostly to pitch. Scott caught for me in Virginia. He said that I was good. I was beginning to practice pitching more, and more pitches on top of the fastball, perhaps beginning to develop a muscle memory playing baseball.

At the end of the week, we said goodbye to everyone. Instead of driving through the night, we left early in the morning and drove back all day. I fell asleep after we set off on the road, and I continued to sleep for much of the way between rest stops. The entire time I held onto my big purple prize.

Chapter 15

There were two Andrews in my third-grade class, and our last names both started with the letter T. We went by our first and last names in class for a day. Then our teacher, Mrs. Mankowski, asked me about going by Andy in class. That was all right. I thought of my father's friend and his cottage at the lake. He had called me Andy before then. We had gone back to his cottage on July 4 and had a great time. There was an inflatable raft floating on the water. Everyone that was there the first time was there again. Someone had made homemade firecrackers, and when they were set off in the sand, they made a muffled thump and a small hole or crater above the water's edge. We plugged our ears and watched from the chairs or the dock. We were otherwise in the water for most of the day. Alex and I played on the inflatable raft. We wrestled and practiced football in a way by trying to knock each other off into the water. There was no punching or kicking, but we were blocking and tackling, of course. Tessa and some other girls sat on the beach under the trees, or rather under the sun. I stayed with Alex and Shawn in the water or on the raft or at the rock right by the raft for most of the day. I had also gone up to Gwynn's lake house again over the summer. We went fly fishing in the middle of the lake and caught a few trout. Off the dock at his house, we caught many crayfish and set them in a fish tank. They crawled around, over the rocks that we had placed at the bottom, and on the small log too. Later that day we put them into the lake. We went to the beach sometimes that summer, to the mountains to go hiking, and to the amusement parks. I told this to my class in the third grade when we were back in school, when Mrs. Mankowski asked what we had done for fun over summer vacation.

We used a device in class that was like a laptop, but it did not have an internet browser or applications for software or games, all it had was a keyboard and a screen, it was a bulky green electronic device, almost like some sort of calculator, but just for a part of one lesson during one of the blocks. Our teacher had to sign out a cart full of them for our class to use. We each got one. They were made for schools and for kids to practice typing. We learned where to place our hands on the keyboard and how to type efficiently.

I continued to get injured sometimes, mostly minor injuries, even in school. It happened one time when we were writing on the electronic devices. Our teacher sat at her desk. When we finished our work, we had to go up and show her everything. I waited in line. Then, when it was my turn, I placed the device on her desk, and as he was leaving, Ronsley knocked it off with his waist. I went to pick it up. I leaned down, and then as I stood up, my forehead hit the corner of her desk. I felt it, that her desk was sharp. I began going through my typography. You see, it flows. "Wait, Andy!" said Mrs. Mankowski.

"What," I said.

I felt a dribble down my forehead, then my nose.

"Someone, get paper towels!"

Gina got up. She came to me with some paper towels. She cracked her fingers and watched in awe as I tilted my head back and applied pressure to my forehead. Our teacher let me sit in her chair while she called the nurse. I held the paper towels to my forehead, and then a minute later the nurse came and brought me to her office. There was a small gash on my forehead.

Not long after that my mother picked me up from school. She took me to the doctor's office, and the gash was sealed with stitches. The doctor said, "Give it a week or two to heal. You're all good to go, Andrew."

I walked out of the office and went to the car. The school day had ended, and I did schoolwork at the house that afternoon. Harry Potter had a scar on his forehead, and mine was almost like his.

There were a few buildings in the school system designated for classrooms. Most were in the same vicinity. In the third grade we had our own school building, baseball fields, a playground. Whether Ned was in our grade or not, he was in our school. He still rode my bus then, and he was always sitting in his seat up front well before anyone else got on the bus. Sometimes the bus driver was somewhere else. He was just there looking out the window. Other than that, I sometimes saw him outside at recess. Then one day I walked into the bathroom during break, and he was sitting with his pants down on, or in that case in, a urinal. He looked at me. He did not move off the urinal. But he smiled. He clapped his hands and made several high-pitched noises. I turned around and left the bathroom. His helper was waiting in the hall. I walked by her and got a drink from the water fountain.

It was still breaktime when I got back to class. I went up to my friend Levi. "Guess what was just happening in the bathroom."

"What?"

"Ned was pooping in the urinal."

"Ned?"

"Yeah, he sits up front on my bus. Remember?"

"Ah, Ned!" Levi burst out laughing. "Yeah, that's odd."

We told a few other boys about it. Then they went to the bathroom to see if he was still in there. He was not, but there were paper towels in the urinal, apparently.

Levi lived close to the school. Some days I went over to his house. But most days I went to my house, and after playing sports and doing schoolwork, I watched tv, went on the computer, or played games on a console between intervals of reading. They were all either action or adventure games. The snowboarding game was my favorite, racing the player through the Alps and scoring points by doing tricks. I wanted to learn how to snowboard. I went over to Levi's house and we made homemade pizza and pitchers of Kool-Aid. We went over to each other's houses after school or on weekends. Outside we threw Pop-Its on the ground and played airsoft sometimes, or else Nerf and miniature basketball inside. The first snowfall happened in mid to late November, and that was unusual. By Thanksgiving Day, the snow at the house had melted. That year, many relatives came over, my mother's parents and my father's parents, and some of their siblings. Everyone ate well, the full spread. I played my adventure video game and wished for more snow and for the mountains to open, and then come Christmas, for my own snowboard.

My neighbors across the street had a chalet just down the road from a ski mountain. We had skied there a few times during the previous two winters. It was about an hour away, the lift lines moved fast, and as simple as the runs were, they were all exciting. You could go down the same trail every time and each subsequent run might be better than the last, and you get to know all the bumps, jumps, rocks, patches of ice, the side trails, which one to go down, and where to go for the best experience. Each one is different.

Most of the time, at that point, only my brother and I went up to the mountain to go skiing. Then at the beginning of winter, my neighbors went on vacation, and they invited us to stay at the chalet for the weekend. A few days earlier I had gotten a snowboard. I wanted to try it out, break in my boots and bindings, turn and glide on my board. The first run that we took, down an easy tail, I fell every so often. I got back up, balanced, made it further down the trail. We stuck to the same chairlift and the same three easy trails. I learned the terrain, my balance improved, I carved well and stopped falling in and between turns, then altogether. I practiced, determined to be good. We went up other chairlifts, tried other trails. I fell, got back up. Went off a jump, got the wind knocked out of me. My brother took pictures and videos as I rode through the terrain park. I went over small jumps, touched the edge of my snowboard in air. And then I relaxed. I rode down the trails, that's all. Up the chairlift and down again, through the terrain park and then to the lodge. We went back to the chalet. I learned how to snowboard.

And I continued to practice in the front yard at my house. We piled up a big mound of snow, and I rode down the sides of it. If it was light out, I was outside snowboarding. The neighborhood kids liked that. We all built mounds of snow and small jumps, then invited each other over to try them out on sleds or snowboards. Sometimes, we only played king of the hill. That was best to play at the cul-de-sac. After a snowstorm, the snowplow pushed all the snow on the street into one big pile, and to us, it was like a mountain. Kids were pushed off, or we did flips and spins off the top, sometimes landing on the pavement. With fresh snow, we flopped onto a blanket of it, sprawled out on the surface, and even made snow angels. Then at some point after dark we all went back to our houses. I made hot chocolate. I sipped it, then sat on the couch by the fireplace and hoped for a snow day in the morrow.

Chapter 16

Every year we went on a few field trips. Most of the time they were somewhere nearby, and those outings were a nice digression from the regular school day, but I enjoyed going to Boston the most. A few classes went. They packed us on a bus and dropped us off at the Museum of Science. In the past we had gone inside and studied the exhibits. There were many to look at, fossils, artifacts, photographs, different displays of science, even one of lightning. They were all works of art, all fascinating, I thought, especially because we were on a field trip. This time we walked along the freedom trail. The chaperones led us around the city. Our group spent the most time, out of any other stop, at Faneuil Hall, and for the most part, inside the candy store. That was popular for my group and most others.

The Red Sox had won the World Series two years earlier. It had been 86 years since the last time that they had won a championship title. Fans were still celebrating, and I was too. The team was good. The store had memorabilia displayed everywhere. Some kids in our group browsed the Red Sox candy. I went up to the case of Gobstoppers. There were a variety of flavors, and they were all packed tight.

I reached in with the prongs and out came three. I gave one to Dana, then bought the other two for myself. We eventually made our way to the North End and stopped at a church. There were other groups and chaperones outside. My friend Julian and I snuck around behind the building. We went across the street into a long courtyard. There was a fountain. I noticed all the coins in the water and wondered how many wishes were floating in the air. We went up to a statue toward the front, facing a busy street. It was of a man, Paul Revere, riding his horse. It seemed brilliant, resolute.

"Look at that horse!"

"My God!"

We ran back to the church. The groups were still outside. Someone was explaining a part of the history of the Old North Church. "He told his comrade to signal by lantern when the British were coming. He might have said, 'Shine one if by land, and two if by sea…' Does anyone know how many lanterns were lit?" A few kids said two.

Ned may have technically been in my class, though he was seldom in the classroom. He came to collect papers and other items, then went off into the specialized classroom in another part of the building. He had a tremendous outburst in the library once. When we were there reading, he came in and ripped books off the shelves and threw several against the walls. Then he just walked out, and we heard a tantrum far off down the hall.

For his birthday, Ned invited everyone in our class to his party. It was at the pool inside our high school. I had swum there on the swim team for a little while, and then I focused on conditioning afoot, on the land sports that I played throughout the year. We all swam in the pool first, then opened presents. Ned jumped off the diving board. He did for much of the time. As we went around yelling, "Marco!" then, "Polo!" he belly-flopped into the water. And he continued, swimming to the ladder, climbing out of the pool, and running back to the diving board, clapping his hands. The belly flops themselves were almost like a mighty applause. We had the pool to ourselves for hours. He opened presents. He got an aerobic exercise ball on which he bounced wildly, and after a while, did handstands and flips. He had a lot of fun. And it was just before the school year ended.

My aunt Gina's boyfriend had a pool at his house. We went to it in the summer. I liked the pool a lot. He had Rolling Stones memorabilia, and the pictures and posters and their logo highly inspired me. Nestor and Weston and their mother went to the pool with us, or to the beach or the lake to go swimming. The pool had a bouncy diving board. I jumped onto the board from the pool deck and bounced into the air. Sometimes I dove into the water, and other times I did tricks mostly spins and flips. We had diving contests. My brother took pictures, or else he swam laps along the side of the pool. He was also on the swim team, had been for several seasons and continued to swim. I stayed busy with land sports. We had football camps throughout the summer. Julian was on the team. After a morning practice one day, we went to a pool. At that time of year, in August, all the wild berries were plump and ripe. There were raspberry and blackberry bushes all throughout wooded areas that had patches of grass or weeds or bare patches open to the sun. We picked and ate many berries. They were all that I had for lunch, and they were good. Our coach encouraged us to eat a lot. Julian invited me over to his house. He said that there was a spot nearby with tons of blackberries. "Let's check it out," he said.

"All right."

We left the pool. My mother dropped us off at his house. Julian got a five-gallon bucket from his garage, then we set off down the road, walking on the side.

"Look, there they are."

"Ooh. I think we'll need a bigger bucket."

Off the side of the road and at the edge of an open field were scores of giant wild blackberry bushes. Some were ten feet tall, plus. All of them reached toward the sky, the sun, right in the open field. We started picking berries. For every couple of berries that I tossed into the bucket I ate one. No cultivated land could produce such succulent fruit, only in the wild. Yet we were in the middle of town, and the spot had enough water from the gully and energy from the sun to produce loads of fruit. We filled the bucket, then walked back to his house. I felt sated, quite full, and I had no room for dinner.

The next day after football camp I went back to the pool. I swam around lightly, wondering about what Julian had done with all those blackberries, if he had made pies or jams, or just ate them. I wore goggles underwater, just as Leanne and I had done at the lake earlier that summer. The water in the pool was clear. In the lake, it was murky. Rays of light shone through the water and in a gentle current freely floating sediment sparkled. We swam around a submerged rock and searched for anything interesting along the lakebed. I thought that she was a mermaid. With only the muffle of underwater sounds and the swish of the wind from above, swimming in golden sunlight among strange underwater lifeforms seemed phenomenal.

Gwynn and I went to Boston at the end of summer. His mother took us there. We walked through the Commons and then through Back Bay. The sun shone through trees dotting the sidewalk, and the street and the brick buildings glowed. I looked upon the setting admirably. We crossed a few streets and went inside a building and then an elevator. We rode up, then got off. I looked out through the windows on every side of the floor, and each view was different. The north-facing view was the most spectacular. From another side, looking down at the rows of apartments and the domed roof of the building next door, I got excited, and vertigo.
"Can we go to Faneuil Hall?" I asked.
"Of course we can."
Gwynn's mother took us on the subway. We got there fast, then went inside the candy store. I wanted to show Gwynn the jumbo Gobstoppers. We both bought one and then started to eat them outside. He went across the street toward a clothing store, and I did too, and then we went inside. He picked out a pair of shorts, tried them on, then wore them up to the counter. The clerk tried reaching across to scan the tag. She could not. Then he hopped up onto the counter. She scanned the tag and asked if he needed a bag, but for his other shorts. After checking out, we walked outside into the afternoon sun.
"Are you boys hungry?"
"Yes!"
We walked through the North End and found a small Italian restaurant on the corner of the block. We sat at a dining table by the front window. We drank water, and the bread that they served by the basket was light and fluffy. In a bowl next to that sat a big knob of garlic, and in another, a pool of olive oil. My diet then permitted bread, garlic, pasta, desert. What became a dietary nightmare tasted delicious. The football season was just around the corner, beginning at the start of the schoolyear, and I had been trying to bulk up. We had a nice lunch.

Around the corner from the restaurant stood Paul Revere's old house. We decided to go and see it after walking outside. The area glowed in the afternoon light, the narrow streets, open spaces, the facades spanning the length of each block.

"Paul Revere's statue is right down the street," I said.

"Really? I want to see it."

"Me too. He's riding his horse."

The house appeared quaint from the exterior, historic and well-preserved. We walked around and went inside. The interior seemed rustic, colonial, contrasting the modern development all around, and all throughout preserving originality while progressing modernity. I pondered that vaguely, even at the statue, and taking the train back to the house.

Chapter 17

My father umpired some of the Little League baseball games. He called balls and strikes. When I was up at bat, the strike zone suddenly enlarged. And when I pitched, it was the opposite, the strike zone seemed smaller. That was when my father umpired my games, and it was the same for other kids whose fathers umpired their games. I was in the Major League. For my first at-bat in the majors, I hit a home run. It was a high fly ball that came down on top of the fence and then bounced over. The field only had a two-hundred-foot max depth, home plate to the center field fence, and that's exactly where the ball came down on, then bounced over. I jogged around the bases, and I thought interesting how the ball had bounced off the fence and went over. It must have been one in a million. All the other fly balls fell short or flew beyond.

My friend from school, Charles, was on my baseball team, and so was my friend from football, Matt. There were maybe a dozen other kids, and I warmed up and played and hung out with them the most. Our team's color was blue, and we were the Cubs. We were good, from the beginning of the season through playoffs. A lot of us practiced often. My top recreation over the summer was playing baseball, pitching at home, batting and fielding at an open field, and after that was football. My father caught for me in the front yard, and he called balls and strikes in the yard too. On the field, I thought that it was almost the same as practicing in the front yard, but with a mound, a whole field behind me, and a batter trying to score, hit a home run. Then at last, it was time to pitch.

We practiced in the afternoon. On sunny days it was sultry. No one brought water. We chewed on sunflower seeds and we were all dehydrated. Matt's mother sometimes watched us practice, even cheered us on as we ran sprints in the heat and more so during games. Those went on all day over the weekend, with some doubleheaders, and several games each week throughout the season.

One of our regular substitute teachers was the seventh-grade baseball coach, Matty. It was not a party in class whenever he was called in, but a fun occasion. Our teacher left packets for us to work on, and most was then homework that night. Charles and I looked forward to seventh grade. We were going to be on the middle school baseball team and Matty was going to be our coach. As our teacher, he tried to spook us by playing scary videos. They were of a seemingly real boogeyman, and it moved slowly, boogying in the dark, which added some suspense amid all kinds of eerie sound effects. It blurred, buzzed, then faded and turned off. We crowded around his desk and computer. One girl went to the cubby area and got a juice pouch. "Kayli's a sissy!" said Ron.

Some classmates picked on Kayli. Charles was the class clown. He went up to Kayli, then let out a fart and said, "Aw, Kayli farted!"

"Charles, sit down in your seat!"

We let out a lot of our energy at recess, on the swings or playing sports. Then we went inside and had read aloud. Our classroom was connected to another classroom but divided by a folding partition wall. Both classes sat together as one teacher read to us. Ben was in the other class. He, Charles and I sat in the back row against the wall. That day Kayli sat crisscrossed on the linoleum floor. The teacher reading aloud calmed me. That block during the day was usually meditative. Then Charles farted, and the kids giggled. Our teacher raised his eyes above the book, then continued reading. The door opened unexpectedly. It slammed against the wall. Ned rushed into the classroom. He went up to our teacher's desk, then picked up a glass bottle and threw it at the floor in front of Kayli's feet. It shattered. "Ned!" our teacher shouted.

His helper came into the room. He yelled, then wailed. Then he ran out of the classroom and down the hall. Everyone stood up from the floor. Kayli checked her legs and feet for wounds. She was fine. Everything was okay. Our teacher swept the glass into a dustpan, then dumped the glass into the trash. Silent reading ended early that day. Ben went back to his classroom. Charles, Zack and

I went into ours. Then the partition doors closed, classes rotated, and I worked on math.

Chapter 18

We drove to Virginia over break again, but this time we stayed at Brenda and Scott's timeshare with my aunts and uncles and cousins. It was at a large resort built on the base of a mountain. Most of the vacations that we went on were similar, at a timeshare or resort, except for the time that we went to Orlando, and we stayed at a hotel, we went to amusement parks, and we visited the world's largest indoor skatepark. At least someone had told me that it was the largest at that time. The skatepark was spread out, dense, and featured a variety of elements for most levels, all located inside of a shopping mall. My parents browsed around while my brother and I rode through the skatepark. I did tricks, and he took pictures. All the elements, even just the ramps, were unlike any that I had been on before. Some people were nearly acrobatic on their skateboards. The facility was full of professionals. They calibrated their trucks and bearings before dropping in a bowl or halfpipe. I rode along the ramps, ground on the rails. The following day we went to St. Augustine. My brother swam in the hotel's pool in the morning. We explored an old fortress with cannons, then went to a museum with natural wonders, underwater and upland artifacts. At night we walked along the beach and watched a few surfers ride the waves. The sun went down, and in the morning our flight departed before it rose again.

In Virginia, Kelsey brought her friend Amy to the timeshare. She was from California, and then she had moved down the road from my cousins. I felt lustful. I was a bit shy at first, but then adventurous. Amy was a hairstylist. Before long she and Kelsey took turns straightening my hair. We were at the resort for a week. Every day the girls straightened my hair. I enjoyed it, and they liked that.

My parents and my brother and I stayed in a condominium on a different street. Every morning I got up and walked to the other condo. Then after that morning routine we all left for one activity or another.

There were many kinds of recreations at the resort. It had a large indoor water park, swimming pools, hot tubs, saunas, arcades, animals, tennis courts, basketball courts, a golf course, a ski resort, and more. Even though it was summer, the ski lifts were open. Some of my relatives had never been on a chairlift before, so we first went to the mountain. It was a chilly, foggy day. Kelsey, Amy, my brother, and I stood in the loading area, then the chair swung around, and we all sat down on it. We went up the mountain.

"This is nice," said Amy.

"You like riding the chairlift?"

"Yeah."

"So you both ski in the winter?"

"I snowboard," I said.

"I do too," said my brother. "Andrew goes after school in the winter. A bus drives him up to the mountain and he goes snowboarding at night."

"Aw, that's fun."

"Look back," said Amy. "The views are really good."

I looked back behind the chairlift. The forest spread out to the horizon and in every direction was lush green foliage. Far off were rolling hills and up close a few mountains of a small range. From the south came a soft breeze. Amy was smooth, and the flatiron combatted the moisture in the air.

At the bottom of the mountain was a general store and out front it had a spot to pan for gemstones. I bought a bag of rocks and minerals, then went outside and dumped its contents into a wooden sieve. I sifted everything in a flowing pool of water. There were all kinds of rough, colorful gemstones, turquoise, blue, purple, and pyrite. I needed inspiration. All that I found were rocks and minerals. I got another bag. Sifting the rocks was fun. I kept the best stones, all very colorful, with exceptional clarity.

Another day we played minigolf, baseball, basketball, and we went rock climbing indoors. We watched movies and went for walks after dinner. Amy was between San Diego and Los Angeles, or in both. Most days we went to the water park. Ever since I had learned to walk and went to amusement parks, I liked water parks the most. The water floated all around, squirting, spraying, splashing, rolling over as waves.

At the indoor water park, there were some of the best waterslides that I had been on, except for the one in Orlando. One of those was like a freefall. You started by going into a small pod on top of a high platform, and for a little while you stood there waiting, then the floor disappeared and you dropped and slid fast down the slide. It seemed to happen all at once. I went on that often.

After a while in the indoor water park, we went in the jacuzzi.

"You like Amy, don't you?"

I sat against the edge. "Yes."

"Come on, lets ride the wave."

We went to the wave. It had a sloped platform that propelled water from the bottom up and over the top, creating a wave. Everyone got a board upon entering. Some people stood on the board and surfed, and others lay on the board and carved. We stood in line.

My brother went first. He caught an edge and fell.

"Right on!" I said.

I went next. The board was slippery. I got on and stayed up. My face kept getting splashed with water, and it was hard to see. I carved from side to side on the wave, surfed on my knees. It seemed like I had been on the wave for a while. Each turn and carve happened in seconds, riding forward, firmly planted, lightly wobbling, seconds were minutes. Then I caught an edge and fell. My board shot back over the slope and landed on the platform. Then I went back, and the force of the water ripped my bathing suit down to my ankles, laying on the deck with water surging back. Was that a wolf whistle? I got up. I went to the lounge area and dried off.

The next day we all left the resort. I kissed Amy. We planned to see everyone else again at Christmas. The drive back to the house was long and the route different than that from their house closer to the coast. I slept along the way, as there were some twists and turns, peaks and troughs, going through the mountains.

At some point shortly after the vacation, my brother went on a mission trip with the church for a week. They assisted a few other churches, did community service, and had potluck dinners. It was an interest of his, I suppose, although we didn't go to church that often. More than that, I figured, it was an experience. It was supposed to be a wholesome mission trip, and it was for the most part. But he got poison ivy at the end of the week, when they were in some patch of woods, and he began to change adversely after that.

Chapter 19

My father's father had passed away over the summer during a period when I had a football camp and sessions were at night. My parents had gone to see him. Along with my grandmother and some of his relatives, they were at his bedside. That day my brother and I stayed at the house while they went to the hospital. He was up in his room, which was where he spent most of the time at the house, and ever since he had gotten back from the mission trip, he was often at the house. The phone rang. I answered.

"How is everything?" I asked.

"It's not good," my mother said. "He has a bad infection in his stomach."

"Oh, no."

"Sorry, hunny. But I have to go. Please check in on your brother."

"Okay."

Later that night I learned that it was a gangrene infection in his stomach—or rather of the gastrointestinal system—and his stomach had become severely bloated. Once I got off the phone with my mother, my aunt Gina called and offered her heart and her sympathy, after learning that my grandfather had passed away. I said, "Thank you." Then I went upstairs to check on my brother. I went into his bedroom. "What's up, Nico?"

"The ceiling," he said.

I looked up. The ceiling was painted white. It was a traditional, rectangular bedroom ceiling. Our bedrooms both had similar dimensions under one-hundred square feet and a layout that could fit a twin or queen bed and two bureaus. I mostly hung out in the basement at the house, especially over the summer, where it was cooler than it was upstairs and along the ceiling were wood rafters and pipes. I said that our parents will be back in the afternoon.

The poison ivy that he had gotten on the mission trip was bad. Doctors had treated it with a steroid medication called Prednisone, and the rash effectively went away, but then we started noticing some changes with his mood, attitude, and alertness. He moved around the house lethargically, and his mind seemed somewhat numb. My parents, I figured, thought that he was going through changes or some kind of phase. But there was something more to it, as though it was microbiological, an alteration of his microbial makeup, the composition of microbiota within the microbiome, a gut-brain connection for him affecting mood, alertness, and vigor. But he had just recovered from poison ivy, and he had only taken an anti-inflammatory medication. So, he rested in his bedroom. And I conditioned well at that football camp, then started the season with vigor.

I was in the sixth grade then. My brother and I went to school at the same time. We rode the same bus. Gwynn met us at the end of our driveway and the three of us walked up the street together. Sometimes Nico walked lagging behind us a little way. We were in middle school, and he was in high school. Getting ready in the morning at the house could be troubling. My mother, my brother, and I left the house at the same time, and we woke up at the same time too. My mother showered first, then my brother did, and then I went last. I sometimes did exercises while waiting to use the bathroom, pushups or sit-ups on my bedroom floor in the sliver of space beside the foot of my bed and the wall.

One morning after getting ready for the day I was making breakfast in the kitchen. I poured cereal into a bowl and then added milk. I noticed that my brother had been in the bathroom for a while. I thought about yelling up to him. Then, finally, he walked downstairs. Something seemed very different, but I did not realize what it was at first. He came into the kitchen. He had no eyelashes.

I dropped my spoon into the bowl. "Uh."

Nico blinked.

"Are you going to school today?" I asked.

"I... don't think so."

"Okay. Get mom to call you out."

He walked back upstairs and went to our parents' bedroom. Soon after my mother came down and wished me a good day at school and practice.

The doctor said that his eyelashes might grow back, or they might not. But, surprisingly fast, they grew back. That had quickly followed his poison ivy, and it happened all at once. Later it seemed like his psyche was beginning to be affected. His skin became dry, he developed eczema, and he seemed to be dehydrated.

"You need to drink more water, Nico," I said. I stayed hydrated. I drank water or sports drinks throughout the day, and on ordinary days I had school, then practices or games, with sometimes the latter on the weekends. That was my usual day in the sixth grade. But there were then more unusual, unordinary days for my brother, and in turn for me, throughout middle school and high school after he had gotten poison ivy.

Chapter 20

That all began to transpire, and the stress in my brother's psyche exacerbate, during the middle of the Great Recession. Every day my parents were worried about the economy. We ate Hamburger Helper for dinner, I had peanut butter and jelly sandwiches for lunch, and occasionally canned ravioli for one or the other. Of course, there was more variation to lunch and dinner than that. Sometimes we had rice pilaf as a side dish, curry, couscous, carrots, and broccoli. During the spring and summer, we may have even had cookouts on the deck occasionally. But it was a troubling period. I began to develop an interest in investing. My grandparents, Nana and Papa, had invested heavily in the stock market. They did well with their investments. My father said, "Now's the time to buy stocks." "The market will bounce back." So, I did some research. I did not use derivatives or algorithms, but some intuition. One company seemed promising in the stock market, Amazon. I liked the company name, its stock price was low, and there was anticipation of having a positive return on investment. The following day, I used some money from my bank account to purchase company stock. My father matched the stocks that I bought. "This is good. Diversify your portfolio," he told me.

Every day I checked Amazon's stock price. When it was higher than my buying price, I got excited. I enjoyed learning beyond the curriculum in school, trading in the stock market, playing sports, making creations of art, and more to each area of study. Upon getting back to the house in the afternoon or evening, I worked at the computer desk, on a coffee table, or on my bedside in a notebook.

My brother and I were distant at that point. He still often stayed in his bedroom at the house. It was football season for me. I out of the house most of the time. During the week, I went to school for the day and then to practice for a couple hours after. Saturdays we had games, and Sundays were our days off. I met Nick one practice at the beginning of the season. It was his first year playing football. He had gone to our school until the third grade, but we were never in the same class, and then he moved to Costa Rica for a couple years.

"Nice to meet you, Nick," I said. "I'm Andrew."

"Let's play football," he said.

We had many classes together the following year, in the seventh grade, and we became good friends.

In middle school we had three terms, trimesters, and our schooldays and studies varied much more than the previous schoolyears had. About halfway through the sixth grade, I got a cell phone. There were many innovations in technology at that time and in the telecommunications industry. Everyone compared phones and exchanged numbers. Anyone whose phone had a touchscreen was looked upon with admiration. I had an LG Dare, a knight-errant. Another popular phone was the Motorola Razr, a flip phone even thinner than mine. And there were many other makes and models too, with limited functions then, mostly calls and texts, but were highly innovative. No one could use their phones in class. That was key.

Some of our classes were hands-on, and in one of those we had to use creativity, intellect, and craft throughout the year. It was woodshop. I used abstract shapes with even some flair in the assignments and projects. Our teacher got excited over wood, and I did too for the class. It was in the afternoon, and I liked to wind down with that class after studying the core subjects in the morning and early afternoon. Everyone liked when the teacher said, "*Balsa.*" And sometimes, "*Balsa!*" We made objects out of wood, *balsa* wood, at first. Mine were three-dimensional shapes and some of those were abstract but none had curved surfaces. We spent many of the classes in the classroom, having lectures, doing worksheets and working on graph paper, until we started working on our final projects and we went into the workshop. Both rooms smelled of new wood. Charles was in the class. Kids used cell phones above the desks.

"Hey!" the teacher said. "What's that gadget?"

"Aw."

"No electronic devices!"

Charles relieved himself a loud one. "*Aw*, Mick farted!"

Some kids laughed, and the new wood smell seemed to expand.

There were not often disruptions in our classes, but there was a plethora more instances, and they tended to happen in succession, were sometimes humorous, even Ned's.

My last class for the day was Spanish. We all chose Latin names or variations at the beginning of the year, and we were addressed by those names instead of our birth names. We all fit our chosen names well, just as we all fit our birth names naturally. Imagining someone with a different name may seem unusual. It is almost as though one grows into their name from birth. Anyway, my name in Spanish class that year was Vinny, and that forename was popular and fit me well.

There was a miniature basketball hoop hanging on the door in our classroom. We used it often. During some exercises, if we were called on and answered the question correctly, we shot the miniature basketball at the hoop. Other times we passed the ball around the classroom and answered questions on vocabulary, tenses, geography, trivia, and more in an interactive manner. It circled the room once, and then I received the basketball. After answering a trivia question, the teacher gestured with her hands that she was open and to pass the ball to her. I flicked my wrist, holding onto the basketball, then flicked my wrist again and the ball flung out of my hand and bounced off her chest back to me.

"Vinny!" she said. Gina and Dana both let out great guffaws. She smiled. "You like to play basketball, Vincent?"

"Yes."

And that flick pass became everyone's favorite basketball move in class. People flicked their wrists, then laughed. Our teacher played more on the miniature basketball hoop after that. I later got one for my bedroom door and played basketball before going to bed. But it was autumn then, and during that time at night I went over football, getting ready for game days on Saturday mornings.

Chapter 21

When we drove to Virginia for Christmas, about halfway my brother began singing aloud. We were all in a full compact car, and we had been on the road since 5:00 a.m. When I asked Nico to stop singing, he sang louder. I looked out the window. My parents turned down the radio and he gradually relaxed his vocals and stopped singing.

Then he started again. I took out my phone. There was little to do on it then except for calling and texting. It didn't have games or applications, and most of the early smart phones didn't either. Those advancements were in development. I began texting Charles, and then I thought of Gina, but I texted Dana. "Will you go out with me?" I smiled. I was in the sixth grade. Then I wondered, wait, to the movies? We went back and forth for a little while. The rest of the drive was smooth, not too noisy.

I went straight inside the house when we arrived in Virginia and greeted all the relatives. We wished each other a Merry Christmas. My aunt asked how I had been, and about middle school and sports.

"I've been good," I said. "And it's going well. Are Kyle, Kelsey, and Matt in the house?"

"Great! Yes, they're upstairs. Go up and say hello."

So, I went up to the big room above the garage. I told Kelsey about the car ride.

"Aw, what did she say?"

"She likes romantic comedies."

That evening, we all watched a comedy movie on tv. Most of the channels played old school holiday movies, and many of those delighted me. I went to bed after that. The long car ride had been tiring. The next day, I went outside and saw that the weather was mild. There had been a blanket of snow on the ground at my house, so I took advantage of the day by playing sports in the front yard and basketball on the driveway, in the cool breeze and in the morning and midday sun.

While we were in Virginia, my brother almost completely changed, and in a way that was opposite the car ride. It might have been that he did not sleep well or much at all. He was lethargic again, and more apathetic than he had been before. My parents were concerned and noticed more than anyone else, except for me. But I still had a nice week, and I wished that his was good too. I went on walks around the neighborhood with Kyle and Kelsey. On Christmas Eve, we lined both sides of the street with translucent paper bags and placed small candles inside each bag and then at night we lit the candles along with everyone else in the neighborhood, and the dim, candlelit streets, faintly flickering altogether appeared light and airy. It was a holiday tradition, and it looked spectacular. Then they let fly some sky lanterns. They floated up and into the atmosphere. We watched from the driveway. The candle display along the street shone with the Christmas lights and decorations. It was vacation, and Christmas Eve. I enjoyed every moment. But it seemed like my brother was distant.

I had signed up for the afterschool ski program earlier that year. When we returned to school in January, the ski program began. There were about twenty-five kids altogether. We went to the mountain in a motorcoach after school on Wednesdays. Every grade in the school district was let out of school an hour early on Wednesdays, and for the rest of the afternoon and night on those Wednesdays in the winter, we skied or rode snowboards at a mountain about an hour away. The slopes were usually open and had few other skiers or riders that were not on a ski team or doing a ski program, but some afternoons the trails were crowded. I sat toward the back of the bus with a group of others in the sixth grade. I reclined my seat. I thought that Gudrun was kind of funny, with her pillow, and bringing her pillow on the bus.

An hour later we were dropped off at the ski lodge. Joe, Nick, Ryan and I snowboarded together and we often rode with others in our grade. We often went through a small terrain park. On the way there we had to cut across a trail. Joe and Nick went ahead of me. It was toward the end of the night. The setting was quiet, mellow, illuminated by lights set atop scattered telephone poles along the edge of the trails and the moon. As I was going down and across a trail, a kid crashed right into me from the trail above. I fell, and while lying atop the snow on my front, I watched a girl from the program ride straight at me. She tried to stop but not fully. She slid fast, and then the edge of her snowboard hit my mouth. Everything went black for a moment. My canine tooth went through the right side of my lip. She rode on. I got up, then I went down the mountain. Joe and Nick were at the chairlift. They were waiting for me with some of the girls.

"I'm going into the lodge," I said.

They all looked worried. My mouth was bleeding. Both boys got out of the lift line and went with me into the lodge. I found the first aid office. Ski patrol called for help. Then a medic brought me to the hospital. He dropped me off, and right away, a nurse led me into a room. My parents arrived just as the doctor stitched my lip back together. It took him only ten minutes to finish, and after that, we all left. In the morning, my mother brought me to see the dentist.

"So, the same tooth of the anterior. How did that happen this time?"

"Snowboarding."

"I'm a skier."

"I like skiing," I said.

"Yes, now let's fix that tooth."

By February break the injury hardly seemed noticeable. My brother and I both had birthdays in February. He still seemed low, drained, and had ever since his mission trip and getting poison ivy earlier that year. We celebrated our birthdays on the same day with family. It was usually on the first Sunday of break. We ate lasagna and meatballs for the big meal. My father cooked in the kitchen. Almost everyone ate at the dining room table once the food was ready, but a few people stayed in their seats at the bar in the kitchen. My mother sat in front of her big bowl of salad. She said,

"Den, you forgot the garlic bread!" He went to check. He opened the oven, smoke poured out.

We all ate the lasagna and meatballs and had bread rolls. It was delicious, and it may have been then or sometime around then, thinking of all the allium and wheat in that meal, when the smooth muscles of my abdomen first began to prickle after eating.

My mother said, "Ma, Andrew bought some stocks a little while ago."

"That's great," said Nana. "You hear that, Jerry?"

"What?" said Papa.

"Andrew bought some stocks."

"Stocks. That's good to."

They had gotten into the stock market long before then. It was my twelfth birthday. I knew that I was getting older. Nana and Papa, though I didn't realize it, were getting older but maybe growing closer together.

Later in the afternoon everyone ate dessert. Gina brought a raspberry vanilla cake with buttercream frosting, and I ate a lot of it.

My mother asked, "Does anyone want some tea?"

"Yes, please."

"Yes, thank you."

"Does anyone else want tea?"

My grandmother and my aunt said that they did. So, she filled the tea kettle and set it on the stove. Five minutes later it started to whistle, and this noise must have triggered something in my brother, the light of a neuron. Then, at once, he began singing, "Tea for two, two for tea, tea for two," and so on. He sang only those two lines.

"Stop it," I said.

"Now that Dottie's not with us I'm singing the song."

He carried on. "Tea for two, two for tea, tea for two." And so forth.

Chapter 22

The next several weeks and then months were full of my brother's languish yet hyperactive fret at the house. He moved around the first floor and upstairs lethargically, moping about, as I had thought. He may have been drained physically through neurological phenomena. I was either out of the house or down in the basement, otherwise frustrated at his change in character. That all happened somewhat gradually over a year or so, since his mission trip, a period of highs and lows, or rather periods of being highly lethargic and fretful and periods of being more relaxed, eased, his normal self, body, and mind then. I began to go through puberty at that time. I played sports every season. It was springtime, nearly the end of the school year, and the middle of the baseball season. When I pitched, I felt at ease, relaxed and composed. I had a uniform wind-up on the mound, except for going from the stretch, and threw mostly fastballs and later added more breaking balls and changeups to the rotation. It was my last year in Little League. Middle school baseball started in the seventh grade, and so did middle school football. Matt and I were still teammates in the Major League. Through the summer we played football together. And sometimes we played airsoft at Sam and Will's house. They had a big yard, an outdoor pool, and behind that was a large wooded area in which we played football or wiffleball, pool games, or airsoft games respectively. Alex often went to their house and sometimes Chris, Matt, and I went too, and when we all got together and played in the yard, woods, or pool, excitement, enthusiasm and camaraderie were woven into the day. At the end of every game in the yard or the woods, we walked back to the house and went over the upcoming schoolyear, sports, field trips. After playing outside all day, we often went for a swim. I had some body hair, though sparsely grown, and I could grow facial hair around my jawline and chin. Everyone was developing, body and mind, physically, creatively, analytically.

Before then, throughout childhood and adolescence, I had hung out with Alex and Chris a lot, playing in the street or on our driveways. We lived in the same neighborhood. When there was no snow on the ground, we rode skateboards, bikes, and rollerblades around the neighborhood and sometimes on ramps in our driveways. Or we set up ramps on the street and rode on those for hours. We fell all the time, and some of the falls were mighty wipeouts, but we always got up. We were much better than we thought we were. There was a stream that ran through the neighborhood, and on their street beside the road was a small ravine with a gradual slope and enough space between that and the water to use the spot for biking. We placed a ramp toward the bottom of the slope and then rode down the ravine and went off the ramp. We tried to get the most time in the air as possible, or if we were feeling brave, to land the best trick. We soared through the air. One time I tried letting go of the handlebars on my bike in midair. But I wobbled a lot, in midair. I lost balance, landed on the ground back wheel first, then stopped along the flat ground. I sighed, the wind undulated out of me. I walked back up and rode down the slope and went off the jump again. We kept at it all day until it got dark outside, then we went inside.

On those days throughout the year, I either went back to my house or went inside for dinner at around six at night. My brother had thinned down to about one-hundred and ten pounds, whereas I weighed on average between one-hundred and forty to one-hundred and fifty pounds from season to season that schoolyear. He seldom ate or slept. My parents brought him to see a doctor, and he was administered medication for his mood that had light, sedative effects, but it may have adversely affected him, instead of aiding his mood and his sleep and eating schedule. Altogether, mine was fuller then than it had been before. I was busy with school and sports after school, and I hung out with friends or expanded my creativity through reading, drawing, even puzzle-making-or-solving during free time: jigsaw puzzles, crossword puzzles, Sudoku, et cetera.

In the fall, we went to Vermont on a little family getaway. My father drove us after school on Friday. It was the weekend after our football season ended, but the weather was mild and warmer than it had been for many of the days through which we had played at the end of the season. My brother was quiet on the drive, and he seemed even tranquil as we drove along the countryside, the hills and mountains, under the canopies of trees and the afternoon light filtered through. We were going to spend the weekend with my aunt Brenda and uncle Scott. They had a timeshare in Stowe, and we were staying with them in their condo. All around were forests and mountains with large slabs of rock and deciduous trees, pines and evergreens. Most leaves had already yellowed, and some had reddened, both radiant in the warm sun, the quaint landscape. The outdoor pool in which later my brother swam was still open. That was vital to him, a good swim. I swam in the pool too, but it was more of a thrill when I swam in the river.

The following morning, we went into town to an art show. It was in a big field and there were many displays. Under large open tents stood vendors, artists, paintings, sculptures, and reproductions. My mother admired the *Mona Lisa*, but I liked the *Girl with a Pearl Earring*. Posed in proportion to the golden ratio, she charmed me through the canvas, my passion through the beauty and balance of it all.

When we got back to the condo, Brenda and Scott brought us all biking along a path that followed a river. The path was paved smooth and wound through wooded areas beside which meadows were set, and behind those stood trees rising with the elevation gain toward the clear sky, cottoned clouds, and the sun. It smelled fresh going beside the grass fields to the left, and the autumn setting bucolic. The river flowed to the right, the water sparkled and looked pure. On our way back, we stopped at an open area beside the river.

"Scott," I said. "I'll go in the water if you go in."

We all stood on the rocky bank. I took off my clothes and then dove out into the river. It felt good. I floated in the current, and in some parts, the water seemed quite deep. I ducked under and touched the bottom, then surfaced. Then I heard a splash behind me. Scott was in the water. We floated downriver.

"Pretty nice, right?"

"Refreshing!"

Ten minutes later we rode our bikes back to the condo. I could have swum in the river a bit longer, but they wanted to get back for a snack, and I to practice baseball. Scott and I went outside in the backyard. I pitched to him, and he called balls and strikes. The bike ride and the quick swim was my warmup. By then I could throw a few different pitches. They looked good. Scott said that my breaking ball had a lot of movement.

I tossed the ball up, caught it, then got set, wound up and threw a strike. After my brother began going through his hardship, I became more introspective, associative, and though frustrated, easygoing, trying to carry the same composure that I had on the pitcher's mound to other sports, activities, and studies. We were only practicing on the grass, and we continued until the sun went down, then went inside for dinner.

The next day we toured an ice cream factory. We got free samples, and then we left and saw the countryside and stopped once more for some fresh made cheese. Then, driving back to the house, my brother started up again.

Chapter 23

Middle school baseball progressed everyone's athleticism in the sport, everyone's concentration and style while playing, focus and coordination too. In Little League we played every position, and in the seventh grade we had primary positions and a batting lineup, honing in on our skills in the field. Ryan played first base. I played third base. And Charles sometimes played at second base. Then when I pitched, he played third base. Many baseball players that year played club hockey during the season instead. In any case, we were still good, in the field and at bat. Throughout the entire season, I never made an error at third base. Our coach said, "The kid doesn't miss a ground ball."

On days between games, we had an hour to ourselves after school ended and before practice started. Some of us walked to the store and bought gum and sunflower seeds. We were adolescents in middle school at that point, but we still rode the swings on the elementary school playground. From there we saw the entrance to the school. Someone always watched for our coaches to turn the corner and drive in. It was usually Harry. "Here they come," he said. And then they pulled up to the curb, my old substitute teacher and his father. We had to unload the equipment out of their truck, all the bat bags, helmets, buckets of balls, catcher's gear, tees, and more. I picked up a couple of buckets of balls. Harry carried the biggest bags, the catcher's gear. His parents were lobbyists, and he did the tough chores around the house, chopping and stacking wood, shoveling, and mowing the grass. Or at least they were the same kind of chores that I did at my house, if my father didn't finish them first. Harry and Nick were neighbors, and they lived by the ocean in a coastal neighborhood. John, who normally played baseball but had played club hockey that year instead, lived down the street from them. And Matt, who was in the grade below our's, was a short walk down the road. I went over to Nick's house on the weekends, sometimes after school between seasons, and usually with John. We hung out in the fall and then more frequently in the winter. They both skied, and I was going to ski, I had told them. I still liked being out of the house. It was a mystery how my brother might be from day to day, his mood and his frame of mind as he was undergoing changes, whereas I always counted on myself being full of energy and mentally sharp. He and Nick's sister were the same age. They may have even been in the same class in one of the early grades. He had changed a lot since then, worried and fret frequently too, after he had gone on the mission trip and his mind and body began to alter. Mine was at its childhood peak of filling out, as both were still developing.

Throughout the year our school put on a few dances. They were on Friday nights. We always went to them. It was something different to do apart from schoolwork, sports, or hanging out. Many kids anticipated the dances with excitement. I went to most of them, and I regarded the dances more casually. I danced with Gina, Dana, and Maddy. There were slow-dance songs. For those, a few classic songs were usually played, by Aerosmith, Led Zeppelin, and Journey. Even though my mind was preoccupied with the issues at the house—my brother's afflictions, and I was preoccupied with those often just at the house—I liked the songs, and I liked dancing with the girls.

So, I went to Nick's house afterwards. His sister asked, "Did Andrew dance with Maddy?"

And I said, "Yes!"

"How was it?"

My hands were on her hips, and hers on my shoulders, and we swayed to the rhythm. "Fun," I said.

The next day Nick and I went skiing at a mountain resort with eight mountain peaks, Sunday River. It was November and only twelve trails were open that early in the season. I had not skied in a while and had almost forgotten how to turn on skis. Nick waited for me on the side of the trail as my muscle memory and coordination for skiing came back. After a couple runs, he and I were flitting through the crowds on the slopes, smoothly and suavely. We went past a group of snowboarders on a flat surface.

They each undid their back bindings, then moved across the snow as though they were maimed sasquatches.

"See T, aren't you glad you switched back to skiing?"

"Hey that's part of snowboarding... But yes, I am!"

John had a cabin by a big pond that was close to the ski resort. He and Nick and I stayed there for a weekend later in the season. Their fathers brought us. Just after we arrived, John said that his father wanted to write a book, and I remembered that I had too. I had taken to arts and sciences in school, and math. Writing may come as a craft first, and then a crafted skill. I had written mostly five-paragraph essays in school up to then, or essays with three main points. Later I tried to hone in on that and expand to other styles.

Their cabin sat up a small slope from the water's edge between patches of trees and off a dirt road. I thought that in the summer it must be calm, quiet and quaint with the summer wildlife, the placid water reflecting the sky and the project underway. We walked along the road at night, planning for the next day's ski trip.

We left the cabin early in the morning and parked at the White Cap Lodge. The mountain had just opened, but I could not see anyone on the trails. We bought tickets, then dressed and went outside. We stepped into our ski binding and went up the chairlift. We were the first skiers on the mountain. We took a warm-up run, then cut over to the peak's main chairlift. We rode up to the summit and then skied down the namesake trail below. The conditions were icy, and the trail was steep. It was tough to carve, but the wind blew right at us and slowed me down as I took longer turns either way to the horizontal, my first time skiing on a double black diamond trail. I made it to the bottom and got in the lift line with John and Nick.

With eight mountain peaks and a variety of trails on each one, we wanted to ski as much of the terrain as we could throughout the day. We were on White Cap, the peak furthest to the left, and our plan was to make our way across the resort, skiing on all eight peaks along the way, to one of our favorite trails located furthest to the right on the furthest peak to the right. So, we went rightward, up the chairlift and then skied down to the chairlift of the neighboring peak. We watched the ski racers practicing, gliding down the trail, carving atop the snow, the crisp, smooth noise with each turn echoing from their tracks.

Getting on the next chairlift, we went directly over a small pond partially covered by a net. Someone had already dropped their ski pole onto it. We watched people in the terrain park. They did flips, spins, grinds, and sometimes others wiped out. Some riders stayed in the terrain park all day, freestyle skiing or snowboarding, starting at the top by the entrance or right above one of their favorite features, then going down the course performing tricks, and at the bottom, hiking back up to the top or to the same or different feature.

We then went through a glade. The snow felt soft and fluffy ungroomed beneath the canopy of trees through which I skied. A recent snowfall had covered and leveled some of the moguls that had previously formed on the trail. I searched for drops, small ledges made from mounds on the ground and bedrock. I went off the natural jumps and blanketed moguls throughout the areas of thin tree coverage, and I rode conservatively between the spaces around the denser trees. I was going slow through the glade but keeping up with the others. Sun filtered through the tree trunks and branches; and calmed, the wind blew at us as a breeze. It seemed to lighten as we exited the wooded area and rode down a groomed trail to the next lift. It had both chairs and gondola cabins on the same lift. We got inside one of the cabins and took it up to next peak, thinking that had been the best run so far that day. I was getting hungry. We went up the next quad and skied down and came out at the same trail on which we had skied to cross over to the seventh peak, then went further down on it to the base of the eighth peak. Adjacent to the next trail: Lollapalooza!

We skied in line, then waited to get on the chairlift. I remembered when my brother and I had ridden the same terrain on snowboards. It was different, but an adventure just the same. We raced down the trail and stopped at the lodge for a snack and coffee.

During the first week in June, the entire seventh grade went on a field trip to a small island in the bay after spring sports had ended. We did not have practices or games or schoolwork during the outing. It was a little break from the relative grind at the end of the schoolyear. We stayed on the island for three days. We got on buses at the school and went to the harbor and boarded a ferry. Charles, Will and I stood on the deck looking out over the water. Everyone seemed excited. Around the island, the ocean housed a large ecosystem, and above sea level were trees, plants, zip lines, kayaks, tents, forts, and other long-standing structures on the island.

The three of us were the last students off the boat, taking in the sun and the view of the bay, the other islands and the continental coast. We followed a path across the island to our camping area. Charles and I set our luggage down in a yurt. We unraveled our sleeping bags. Twenty other kids were staying in the yurt. The floor made of wood had groves between each plank. The tarped wall was circular and continuous, except for the entryway, and the ceiling made of the same material was conical.

Outside we followed path overgrowing with plants to a small opening in the trees. It was the edge of the island. We stood on bedrock facing the ocean and directly below was a hidden beach. Straight ahead was another island, with trees growing from its bedrock bent out over the water. It had turned cloudy, and the wind had picked up lightly.

A few teachers were there as chaperones. We did activities and played games to enhance our ecological learning, at the same time using up the energy we had. Fog rolled in late in the afternoon. Someone made a campfire, and we sat around it. Our group was on one end of the island, and the whole grade was scattered around it at every campsite.

At night, Charles and I stepped out of the yurt and walked along the main trail through the island. We went by Will's tent. He was inside, and a few others may have been crammed in there too. Then we heard a far-off call, "*Skee yew!*" Down the main pathway we saw a few other kids, but they had been quiet, they were going back to their tent. They said to check out the old fortress, that that's where they had been, and that it was interesting. So, we went that way. It was in the center of the island, the fortress, and there was a zip line that went hundreds of feet from the top of it across a clearing to a big oak tree at the far end of it. Then we heard the same voice but a different call, "Ay-ay-*ay!*"

Then, "*Arrrrrrriba! Ya-ya-ya-ya!*"

It was Dan Mackey. He was on the zip line, trilling his tongue wildly. We almost fell over laughing. Dan was staying in our yurt, but we did not see him leave that night, nor did we see him leave the following morning. When everyone woke, Dan and his belongings were not in the yurt. His grandfather had passed away the night before, earlier in the evening, and then he found out and took a ferry back to Portland the following morning.

Over the next two days, we rock climbed and kayaked, made food and cleaned up, sat by campfires and played games. Kayaking was adventurous. The water was choppy and around some parts of the island even a bit rough, I thought, almost as though going down rapids. I bobbed over the whitecaps and waves. We were splashed, and mist continuously spritzed us as we looped around, then followed the wind smoothly back to the landing and rode ashore.

Chapter 24

That summer, I went for a run and lifted weights every day, on top of the conditioning sessions for football. Those were at the high school. We ran sprints up a hill, then jogged down the hill, then ran up it again. The perpetual running up and down the hill seemed endless at the end of the sessions. I told myself that we must just have one more sprint, then I will go back to the house, get some water, then some food. But our coach kept saying, "Ready, go!" Now and then a kid sort of collapsed from being winded, or even heaved from the conditioning. I enjoyed either the walk or ride home after the sessions ended, I felt lighter, a bit tired but uplifted. We only had two sessions a week, and for the other five days, I had my own routine at the house. Most of the time I ran on trails to the frog pond, where Gwynn and I had walked out to on pleasant days of youth, and then from the pond I went further along another trail that led to an opening and field near Will's house, and after taking in the sun for a moment I ran back along the trails to my house. In the basement and at the gym, I started to lift weights, bench-pressing, squatting, curling dumbbells, doing push-ups, pull-ups, and sit-ups, while adopting a new diet. Going into the schoolyear I was in shape, and the summer studies maintained intellectual conditioning.

I went to Bill's house one day over the summer with Ben, Charles, and Ryan. He had a large plot of wooded land behind his backyard. We walked out to a campsite where it seemed as though the generation before ours had partied. And we walked around the campsite and explored the wilderness a bit, found old bottle caps, rusted cars, broken glass, golf balls under large pine trees and a bed of pine needles atop the ground.

Then we started going to malls, recreation centers, and outdoor venues. One of our parents dropped us off, and another parent picked us up. We stressed over getting a ride to the mall or to the waterfront or to an ice rink or cinema. Though my parents were stressed, and my brother's afflictions progressed, one of them often brought us or picked us up. We just walked around. I was drawn to some of the artwork on the walls and on the displays. Charles liked to flirt with girls on the outings. One time we brought a group of girls to play laser tag. The place was built inside of an old store, and it had a little arena with fluorescent lights around which we played. Later that night, we went to a Mexican restaurant. The girls exchanged numbers with us. Something I ate upset my stomach. My father picked us up. I sat in the front seat, not realizing that my composition of microbiota had perhaps changed from the conditioning and dieting, and internally bearing the load of the external stresses within the abdomen. The other boys were dropped off before getting back to the house.

Ben and I went to the YMCA in the morning. We lifted weights and ran around the track. He exercised his core as I used the bench press. We switched after each set, then rotated exercises. It was a Sunday morning. Not many others were at the gym.

Down the road was an ice cream store. We went there after finishing our workout.

"Does your sister paint?" I asked.

"Yeah," he said.

I liked Ben's sister and thought that every piece she painted must reflect her beautiful mind. He said that after school someday she might paint me a portrait.

We ate ice cream outside, then we were picked up and dropped off at our houses. Joe was having a party that night. I went to his house in the afternoon. We played lawn games, played catch, went swimming, and made a small bonfire at night and ate smores. After that, I continued eating mindfully, conditioning and training. I played baseball too. In the spring I had joined the Babe Ruth summer league. We did not have practice. We only played in games.

The following week we had a tournament. Our first game was at night. We played at a nice ballpark. Many teammates who had played club sports instead of playing seventh-grade baseball then played in the Babe Ruth league over the summer. Charles's father was the coach. The games were easygoing, being part of the summer league, and we played for fun and to practice, but we played hard and wholeheartedly. I played left field so Charles could play third base. I still pitched, but third base was my favorite spot. I was playing in left field when the game started. My friend Miles, who had played travel hockey in the spring, was our starting pitcher. In the fourth inning we were down by three, the other team was rallying, then I was called in to pitch as a reliever. Most players could only hit fastballs. There was one out. They were at the top of their batting order. I threw six breaking balls and struck out two batters. We rallied the next two innings on offense, and I kept throwing my breaking ball on defense, striking out the sides. In the sixth inning we were up to bat with two outs, down by one. Miles was on second base. I hit a double over the center fielder's head, and Miles scored. Then Charles hit a single and I scored. Mitchell struck out, and the inning ended. We were up by one when we took the field. I struck out the first batter, walked the next, then struck out the third. There were two outs. I threw a fastball, first pitch, and the kid hit a little blooper to center field. Matty-Lo came running in. He made the catch. We won the game.

We lined up at home plate and bumped fists with the other team. Then we took a knee. Coach congratulated us. We had played well under the stadium lights. Our school was athletic. Charles invited me and Mitchell to his family's beach house. It was only a few minutes away, and it was 80 degrees outside with some humidity in the air. About five degrees cooler on the beach, it was a quintessential summer night for swimming in the ocean under the stars. Waves rolled in, then broke on the shore with a soft woosh one after the other.

"This is amazing."

We were jogging along the wet sand.

"Perfect night on the beach."

The next day we ate lunch on the beach. Along with a sandwich, I had cherries, and I ate them like an apple. I nibbled the fruit around the pit and cleaned those dry. I grabbed another cherry, and I bit in and then flushed. My front tooth chipped. I felt it in my mouth, almost like sand or a pebble against other teeth. I took it out and showed the other boys.

"T."

"Yes."

"Your tooth chipped."

"Ah, yes."

An hour later my mother arrived. She brought me to the house. I scheduled an appointment with the dentist for the following day, to fix the same tooth. I went to the office and received local anesthesia around the foretooth. My mouth was numb for a little while after the dentist had finished, but my tooth felt and looked good.

Over the weekend, the baseball tournament continued. On Saturday we had a double-header. I started on the pitcher's mound. My breaking ball was better than ever. I released the ball high, and it went at the batter head level and then curved down right across the strike zone. Not every day did those pitches have that much movement, but during those games that day they curved more than they ever had before. I pitched the whole game and threw a shutout; the other team did not score. We went to our second game that afternoon, ready to play. Charles's father asked if I could pitch again. I said yes. We started the game strong. Then my arm began to wear out. I had thrown many pitches. I walked the same batter twice on back-to-back plate appearances in separate innings toward the end of the game. I struck out the next two batters. It had been a low-scoring second game. We went back to the dugout and rallied on offense in the last inning. We won the game. That day I pitched fourteen innings. And the next day I struggled to even lift my arm. We played a game that night. I stood in left field and watched us lose. The tournament was single-game elimination. Our season was over.

School started at the end of the month. Preseason football began even sooner. I was going into the eighth grade. My brother was in high school. Like many kids at the beginning of middle school, I had been anticipating that schoolyear since middle school began, the classes, sports, extracurricular activities, and being the eldest students in the school.

Chapter 25

My brother seemed to be at ease for a little while. That was when we went to Virginia for Christmas. Our family and our relatives met up again at the resort. We spent the vacation all together in the same condo. It had two floors, two living rooms, four bedrooms, and three bathrooms. It accommodated twelve of us well for the first two nights. Before our trip to Virginia, my brother was overcome with anxiety during the first half of the schoolyear. It was as though his mind was working in overdrive, preoccupied over nonsense. He rattled on at the house, always as I walked in the door after school or sports, and it was often frantic and could have simply been over trivialities. My parents put up with it and tried to assuage him. I went down into the basement as soon as I went inside, feeling frustrated and worried on top of the excitement, joy, and stress of adolescence. I was otherwise kind, generous, and relaxed.

The three primary schools in the district were built on a hill and situated kind of like a campus. The middle school was at the bottom of the hill toward the back. One of the elementary schools was out front and off to the side. And the high school was on top of the hill beside an intersection. In the center of everything was a baseball field, a softball field, an outdoor track, a football field, and a walkway from the high school to the middle school.

One afternoon my brother and I both had biannual dentist appointments, cleanings that happened twice a year. They were scheduled at the same time on the same day. My father, who had worked from home all day, took the afternoon off and picked us up at school. He parked in the middle school parking lot. I walked out to his car and got inside. About fifteen minutes went by. We had seen many high schoolers come down the walkway, the buses leave.

"Well, you both might be late to your appointments."

"What's taking him so long?"

We were just down the hill from the high school, and it was only a short walk away. Maybe he had to stay after class, finish schoolwork or work on homework. Another five minutes passed. And then he came around the corner, moving absurdly slow. Then finally he got into the car. "Why were you walking so slow?" I asked.

"Why were you walking so slow," he repeated, then looked out the window.

We were not late to our appointments. My teeth felt smooth and fresh afterward. I went out to the car.

The drive to Virginia was long and surprisingly pleasant as opposed to the time before. My brother did not sing aloud. My mother rested her feet above the glove compartment. My father drove. And I read a book. It felt like I was moving along the pages with the author, not only moving along the road. We first stopped at Brenda and Scott's house and spent the night there. Then in the morning we drove into the mountains. I rode in the car with my uncle Scott. At some point we listened to a kind of far eastern music. The instrument was played so gently, it reminded me of the wind, the sound of her creation. We pulled into the resort. Off to the right was the water park. I planned to go every day if I could. Scott drove past the entrance and checked in at the main office, and then we made our way to the condo.

The kids slept on the second floor, and the adults slept on the first floor. Kyle, Kelsey, and I went for a walk beside the golf course along a pathway. There were spots of snow on the ground and some ice on the pavement. I slid across the frozen patches on my feet.

"I thought about bringing a little bit of cannabis," said Kyle. "Stepping outside at night. Then going inside. And that Jacuzzi in the bathroom might seem really nice."

"That sounds nice. Would you have had any, Andrew?"

"Possibly."

The next day everyone went to the water park, but only Matt and I went in the water. We rode the slides, sat in the hot tub, floated along the lazy river. Water splashed in our eyes and probably in our mouths. The next day we went to the water park again, and afterward, we went to the arcade and handled ping pong paddles, pool cues, played racing games, and gripped the steering wheels. That night, Matt and I got terribly sick with the flu. Before long we were dry heaving, and it continued all night. The next day almost everyone in the condo got sick too. There was rarely a vacant bathroom. I recovered quickly, after about twelve hours, and it took another twelve hours to get back to strength. But for all the others, that flu spell went on for a few days, trips to the bathroom, cleaning up and eating lots of soup. Only my father and uncle stayed well the whole trip.

We still had a good time and enjoyed the holidays, and then we said goodbye to each other before heading out. My father drove back to the house along a somewhat scenic route. It was quiet and even pleasant. My mother reclined her seat. My brother slept. And I recalled the music and thought of the wind.

Chapter 26

Will invited me to his family's house at the ski resort Sugarloaf for the weekend. They shared it with a few other families, a compact cabin down the road from the village, but that time only Will, his father, and I went. It was my first time at Sugarloaf. Some people said that it was possibly the best ski resort on the east coast. The previous year I had developed skills and a style. That year I began to really enjoy skiing. I even branched out a bit in the terrain park. Will had been skiing all throughout childhood, and he was good. He took long narrow turns down the middle of the trail, or no turns at all and went straight down the trail. He knew how to freestyle ski, but he might have enjoyed racing the most. Some parts of the mountain were more crowded than others, but we avoided the busiest areas and lifts for the most part and got in as many runs as possible.

We went on every chairlift but King Pine, and we skied on every area but the backside of the mountain, which can only be accessed by taking the King Pine lift. The winds were too strong for that chairlift to operate. It was the most thrilling part of the mountain, and with the right conditions, low wind, fresh snow, it can be the best part of the mountain too.

We often went through the terrain park. Will went from feature to feature without stopping. He grinded on rails and spun in the air after going off jumps, landing every time. Every trick was different. One might've been as simple as approaching the ramp backward, going off and rotating halfway in midair, then brushing the rail lightly with his skis and landing forward. And another might have been a classic spread eagle off one jump, then a slow, composed three-hundred-and-sixty-degree rotation off the next. After landing, we met up off to the side of the trail. He told me to get some speed and go off the jump. "All right," I said.

Next run I went off a jump with a low tabletop that curved down into the landing. It felt like I was in the air for a long moment. My arms flailed lightly, and the ground got further away and then came closer coming down the arch. I landed on the slope and skied down to the chairlift. We rode it back up the mountain. Will and I got off the lift and rode down a trail to the left. He led the way through the terrain park and then stopped before the first jump. Our skis had carved through the snow like butter going down the trail, smooth with every turn, and then he dropped in. I did too, and we went off the jump individually but in succession. The launch, the airtime, and the landing were all smooth. We met at the bottom of the trail.

"How was that?"

"Awesome!"

"Right on. You used to freestyle snowboard and could do 360s, right?"

"Yeah."

"Well, try one on skis."

We went back through the terrain park the next run. I went off the jump. I spun in the air, fully rotating three-hundred-and-sixty degrees, then landed on my skis and fell. We repeated the previous run. I tried again and stuck the landing.

Run after run we went through the terrain park, going off jumps, grinding rails, spinning in the air. Then we went up to higher altitudes on the mountain. We rode the T-bar, traversed the slopes, skied through glades, snow with depth, patches of moguls, and over other patches of ice. We went up and down the mountain until the chairlifts closed that day, working up an appetite.

Will suggested getting dinner in the village. He mentioned a restaurant called The Bag. I had heard that they have great pub fare. We went inside. The hostess seated us and asked if we wanted anything to drink. I asked for water. Will ordered soda.

"Pretty soon we can order beer," he said.

The bar was full of skiers and riders. It was warm inside and smelled savory. We browsed the menu. Our waitress came by and asked if we were ready to order.

"I'll order a Bag burger, please."

"Me too," said Will.

"All right, two Bag burgers. Let me know if you want to order anything else."

"Thank you."

She took our menus and went through the dining room. Our plates were served fast. They were completely full—each with a hamburger, curly fries, a cup of house sauce—and quickly we were too. I paid and then we walked outside and went back to the cabin. The following morning, we went out skiing early, and we skied for only half a day before taking the shuttle bus back and driving home in the afternoon.

Chapter 27

Later that year my brother had an awful panic attack. He had been taking a mood medication that seemed to be making his mood worse. Our parents were out for dinner. He came rushing downstairs under a spell of extreme panic and anxiety. There was nothing else wrong. It was a sunny evening. I had been sitting on the couch, then immediately began to try and calm him. He felt like he was dying. He may have had a similar sensation earlier that year and then went the hospital. I recalled that as he sat at the table almost in tears and I told him to lay on the couch and take deep breaths. After a little while, his panic assuaged. I called my parents.

They rushed back to the house. Five minutes later an ambulance arrived. I went down in the basement, and before going to the hospital in one of the cars my mother came down. Distressed, she explained his panic to me, and she believed that his health problems started back when he got poison ivy on his mission trip and then took a steroid medication for it. After that, he may have developed a mood disorder, and the process of trial and error with medications exacerbated his symptoms associated with that. Perhaps as his mind was developing so was his disorder, changing and exacerbating. She repeated that it was a process of trial and error. "He's your brother," she said. "It's not his fault!"

I stayed in the basement for the rest of the night. I remained calm, though worried and a bit shaken up. Earlier that year, I recalled, I had my first experience with his panic at the house. After waking up in the morning, I had begun to get ready for school. I took a shower, dressed, then went downstairs. The TV was on. I poured a bowl of cereal and then sat on the couch. My mother was getting ready upstairs, and coffee was brewing in the kitchen. I had the downstairs to myself. My brother, I thought, must not have come downstairs yet. I figured that my father had kept the TV on.

He left the house for work at 6:00 a.m. I finished my cereal and then went upstairs and brushed my teeth. My brother was not in his room. I checked the basement, and he was not down there either, or in the bathroom, or on the computer. I went outside. The garage door was closed, the lights were off, the windows were down, and it was dark. He was in the car, and the car was on. I went up to the window and knocked to try and get his attention.

"What are you doing?"

I opened the door and turned the car off.

"Did you fall asleep? Come on inside."

We went into the house. He went upstairs, and the panic that then manifested did too. I put on my jacket, then my backpack, and then walked up the street to catch the bus. In school I passed in assignments and started working on those that were due the next day. I ate two lunches, one that I had brought and one from the cafeteria. Each class breezed through its material. The day seemed to go by fast.

I walked home in the afternoon. The hurried rush passed through the front door and side exits. I put on my jacket and went outside and up the hill on the walkway and then to the house. I saw where he had been yesterday, and the sign that said to lead the way. I dropped my backpack and went down to the basement. They were still at the hospital. He had been sedated, they later told me, and he was asleep.

And then I went to sleep. I dreamt of it all that night from a bird's eye view. Earth vividly revolving around the sun, creating a series of images, covering the great period in space. And the orbit it covered, seemingly hypnotic, caused an out-of-body experience. Then focusing in, all that was flowing shone as though in a sea of whitewater, past, present and future morphing into the form of a fractal. Maybe one not infinite but eternal. Fractals are complex patterns that appear to be the same across different scales. They can be, in a way, a form of harmony through geometry that goes on infinitely. To fully see one requires a lens that when focused in or out detects structures and patterns that beforehand were hidden, infinitely reduced in scale or infinitely larger in scale. Its shape has endured for eons, and with it the fractal, the harmony, the creation and continuation. It was not that the hill had no summit; every time that God ascended the summit the universe slipped away and rolled down the hill. To grasp its dimensions the energy must have been immense, creating a fractal, one infinitely small of one infinitely large, which must have been created from energy and that in turn from harmony, and so on eternally, internally, each a world to scale.

A fractal can start from a single line and grow into an infinitely complex pattern, and a lifeform started a branch from a single cell and evolved incessantly to a larger scale. Both harmonize across every scale and period. Progressively the pattern can change, it can evolve, adapt, and branch. A root grows through soil, an idea sprouts in the mind. It may be how consciousness expands, in essence, through a form of energy. The past being kinetic, the future being potential, the present moment is a fleeting glimpse of its combined energy.

I must have woke in a sweat. My mind had been climbing a mountain. I was in the basement. The house had grown darker with the shorter days and the changing seasons. At times I reflected on energy and consciousness. I became more introspective between spells of distress, a bit inward at the house, yet elsewhere I tended to be more outgoing.

Chapter 28

Freshman year of high school began. I had not played football that season or conditioned in the offseason due to injury. In the eighth grade, I had injured my back in a game and played through it but then I had to rest the second half of the season. I thought that I had tweaked it. Sometimes sharp pain diffused through the area around my lower back above the lumbar. I saw a chiropractor until the pain was alleviated and the injury presumably healed without surgery or major readjustment. While playing baseball in the spring, it did not exacerbate, but tweaked, it was not at full strength. Over the summer I mowed lawns. Ryan no longer played football. We got together occasionally while the others had preseason practice and games. I went for a run most days in the morning or in the afternoon. Playing football the following season, I was going to be a running back, and I ran up and down the street or along trails to condition. The distance from my driveway to the end of the street was a quarter mile. I sprinted in one direction and jogged back the other. The trail out to the pond was between a quarter mile and a half mile. On that route I was a running back. I dodged trees, roots, and hurdled branches as though they were players on the ground. I liked that conditioning.

 After school I mowed my neighbor's lawn in the afternoon every couple of weeks. They lived down the street. Their son, and their grandson, had both been my seventh-grade baseball coaches. Their yard was mostly flat and there was only one tree. I was meticulous and after finishing I walked back to the house. Storm clouds had formed in the sky. The air smelled fresh, felt moist and slightly dense. Then a raindrop hit my nose, and still I got ready to go for a run. Soon there was thunder overhead, sheets of rain. It was a torrential downpour, and it started just as I got on the trail. I was no longer a running back maneuvering through trees, but just running through mud and splashing in water. The whole trail was flooded and flowed down to the pond. Through the clearing sat the body of water in ripples. I thought of diving into it and swimming across the pond, but perched on a log by the water's edge was the old snapping turtle. I ran around the outside through tall grass, weeds, and puddles. I followed the trail further into the woods and came out at the field across town. There was a stream at the edge of the woods, normally dry, but then it was flowing with water, surging down the valley and over rocks along the streambed. I ran back to the house. It was so wet. Lightning cracked. Thunder clapped. And then I went inside.

My brother and I were in high school together. There were periods when he was there and when he was not. I usually liked high school regardless. I saw my brother along with everyone else in the hall, as the crowds flowed from class to class. Everyone may have been a bit different outside of their house, but he seemed the same or even gloomier in high school. I tried to stay focused always. He was a senior, and I made the most out of being a freshman.

The seniors had had privileges in high school. They came to school and left throughout the day. They were able to miss study halls, and those periods were usually scheduled at the beginning, middle, or end of the school day. They could arrive an hour later or leave an hour earlier than the underclassman, sometimes two with stacked study halls, and with one in the middle of the day they could have a long lunch. A great decision for many of the students throughout high school—what they were doing after graduation, if they were going to college, and if they were, which college—had already been figured out, and they had begun embarking on the road perhaps before realizing it.

It may seem fractal. The world had always been there from the beginning, and as soon as that one world came to fruition, open and in view, all the other open worlds vanished and new worlds arose, as another world came to fruition, open and in view, with worlds behind, new worlds arise, but there's a fork in the road, and you must get up the hill.

In first period, my teacher asked everyone to write down our goals. It could be for anything, a goal for the class, or that year, or in sports, during college, or even beyond.

She gave us a minute to think. Then she went around the classroom and read some of the goals we had written.

"'Climb Mt. Everest.' That is quite a feat, Danny, and a difficult climb."

"'Get straight As.' Good goal. You are smart, Laura."

"'Score ten goals.' Excellent, Silas. That's a goal within a goal. I'm rooting for you."

"'Design a sailboat.' Yes, I like that. 'And sail along the coast.'"

The day went on and school got out at 2:15 p.m. Normally I went to the house after school. Some days I mowed lawns. I ran or went to the gym, did schoolwork, and I always ate dinner with my family and ended the night in the basement and then went up to bed. One of my goals, which had been one since elementary school, was to write a book. That may have begun on the trails. Though I only read books then, my mind developed further, and intellect began to emerge. Free associations between phenomena formed. Following injury came frustration. An output of consciousness that later came in high school as though in stream had begun to flow. And freshman year had only just begun.

Chapter 29

About a month later the school put on a dance. A group of us got together beforehand. We had heard that the high school dances were unlike those in middle school. There was no slow dancing, it was fast-paced and there weren't many dancing rules. We walked to the high school. There were kids outside the entrance and more inside the auditorium. The place was already full. Most of the freshmen stood off to the side. They all talked, and they seemed a bit timid. Everyone crowded around the floor in front of the stage. For a moment, I got on the stage. I looked out over everyone. There was a crowd of kids grinding against each other. Then I went down to the floor and into the crowd. My spot was right next to the stage. All the older girls stood by the stage or sat on the edge of it. Caroline came to me and then we started dancing. Rick was the DJ. Charles wanted to be up on the stage with him. Later, he did in fact DJ. He played club music mixed with mainstream music, and he sometimes mixed the songs on the stage. There was a cluster of people. The speakers vibrated the floor next to us. After dancing in the crowd, I went off to the side with the others.

Winter came early that year. It started snowing before December. The mountains accumulated the most snow, and everyone who skied or rode snowboards was excited for the season. Some kids started going up to the mountain almost every weekend as soon as fall sports ended. Will had gone skiing over Thanksgiving break, and then over winter break he invited me to his place at the mountain. We left in the morning two days after Christmas and arrived at Sugarloaf midday and that afternoon we went to a gymnasium down the road. Inside it had a skatepark, basketball courts, a gym, rock climbing walls, and trampolines. We jumped on one for at least an hour and performed spectacular tricks. We spun and flipped in the air every bounce. Then we went back to his house. There was a sauna in the backyard built almost like a shed. We went in it that night for half an hour. I first started beading and then dripping sweat. It was warming up. Saunas were exhilarating to me. Inside one my sense of perception seemed slow-motion. The warm, dry wood creaked. The air was full of energy. Then the moment the timer went off, I opened the door and we ran through the snow and went inside the basement and hydrated. I showered, felt refreshed. We ate dinner and then relaxed downstairs. Our skis had been tuned for the trip. We slept in the basement, then woke early in the morning and got dressed, had breakfast, put on our gear and then went out skiing.

During winter, I went to the mountain at least once or twice a month. I tried to go when I had the chance to, and I often stayed for the weekend or longer over breaks. They were vacations not too far from the house. On New Year's Eve there was a dance at the base lodge which we planned to attend, and we wanted to celebrate before and after that too.

Will and I skied all day. We were among the first ones on the lift and then we went down a freshly groomed trail. After a few runs, the lift lines grew, and the mountain crowded. We took only one break to get lunch, then went on skiing the rest of the day and then went to his house and sat in the sauna for thirty minutes again. After that, we went out to dinner. The Bag was full. We got a table and ate and then walked around the village. It was bitter cold outside. We made our way to the base lodge and went inside. There was a group of kids standing by the stairs. It was Nick, and he was with a few others in our grade, Layton, Alex, and Sumner. They were talking to a group of girls. As we walked through the entryway, Will said, "Hey, that's Kristin. You know how I told you we share the house with two other families? She's one of my housemates!"

"Let's go say hi."

We walked over to the circle.

"Ay!"

"Hey guys."

"Andrew, Will!" said Nick. "What are you guys up to."

"We just had dinner."

"This is Isabel, Esme, and Kristin."

"Hi, Will," said Kristin.

"Hey," he replied.

They all seemed cool, and they were pretty. Esme wore a beige headband. Isabel had a little nose ring.

"You boys trying to have desert?" said Layton. "Come join us."

We all went outside and walked along the trail and stopped at the edge of the woods. They had cannabis, and we all tried some of it. The night stilled. The stars and the moon shone vividly bright through the clear sky. We stood in a group. A breeze swept through and then calmed. The girls purred, then pawed at me. Will was talking to Kristin. The others went over their day skiing, the conditions, and the new year. My body had loosened up, felt lighter and warmer. The swaying treetops slowed in motion. It seemed like they were flowing uniformly, interconnected in outline against the night sky. Perhaps an hour passed. Sumner looked at his phone. "It's only been ten minutes!"

Then we walked to the village. Will and I bought snacks. We said goodbye to everyone else and planned to meet up the next day, and then we waited for the shuttle bus. We sat on the bench for a moment. He spaced out. "So that's why Kristin's never at the house," he said. "She stays Esme."

"Yeah, I figured that out," I said.

The next night we went over to Sumner's condo. Everyone from the night before was there. We hung out in the living room and then went to a bedroom and sat on the bed or on the carpeted floor. Esme laid her legs over mine. They were smooth, warm leggings, and her socks were plush.

"What's greater than one," I said. "Two."

"Three!"

"Trifecta T!"

"We're the gewls."

Music played from a loudspeaker. I followed along and then fell back on her legs. Esme poked my shoulder, then my cheek. Then Isabel did. Then the gewls went back and forth, lightly poking me every time. I smiled, amused, and they giggled.

There were soft blankets and pillows around the room, bright lighting throughout, and the fireplace was on. I might have dozed off for a moment. Will shook my arm. "Come on," he said. "We missed the bus."

It was later than I thought. We went back to his house and sat on the couch before going to bed.

We skied the next two days. We saw Matt in the terrain park. He was with a few others from the academy, and they were good. The tricks that they could do were impressive, almost daunting. What we had done on the trampoline they matched on skis. They did flips off jumps, corkscrews, rodeos. They twirled through the air effortlessly. They went off the big jumps. I went off a small jump, spun a full rotation and then landed. Will had much more control in the terrain park but not quite their flair. We met up with Nick, Layton, and Alex. We went all around the mountain and skied down almost every open trail. We saw the girls, or the gewls, and we rode with them until the sun set and the lifts closed for the day.

At night, Will and I got a ride to the village. Alex invited us to his condo. He and Nick met us at the lodge. Outside it was already crowded around the patio area. People were excited. It was New Year's Eve. Nick and Alex led us down a trail, and then we cut through a patch of woods and came out at a road in front of his condo. We went inside and he brought us downstairs to the bottom floor. There were couches, chairs, beds, a big tv, and a few floors above. Alex was new to our school that year. He had moved from Massachusetts, and he lived down the road from Nick. Back in the fall, he and Joe got all worked up at a Friday night football game. That year Joe had transferred to a private high school and they had a top football team. Otherwise he might have been playing on varsity and been on the field then. As a freshman, that's difficult to do. My mind was still carrying my stride in the offseason, and my back felt unscathed after all the skiing, and I supposed that the injury had healed. We all sat on the couch downstairs and then did a cheer to the new year and got ready to leave the condo. We had to bundle up in jackets and had some layers. Then we went outside and across the street and through the woods and up the trail to the village. Layton and Sumner were standing outside by some benches. We all walked further along the trail by the edge of the woods as the festivities were getting ready to begin.

When we walked down to the village at the top of the hour, the area in front of the lodge was completely crowded. Groups of people were coming in. I saw Sam, said hello. He gave me his water bottle. Then I went back to my circle. We had a spot on the outdoor patio, and from there we watched the fireworks. The display lit up the sky and the mountain glowed dim in the background under the moonlight and stars. After the finale, we went inside the lodge. They had arranged a dance for the kids and many were there. Some did not even ski; they were just at the mountain for New Year's Eve. However, the gewls were not at the dance. They had gone to see the fireworks. But I had hoped to dance with them.

Will and I skied the following day. The mountain seemed so open. There were no lift lines. Most people had already gone back to their homes. We went inside the sauna at night, rested, and then left in the morning.

Ryan and Ben were on live, and I told them about the ski trip, the dance and fireworks, the gewls and all the others, and the back medicine. I thought of language and composition, math and sciences. My mind free associated, and I multitasked. I had written ten pages for English. I worked on that, and they played soccer. No schoolwork was due the next day. But it was the last day of break, and I began thinking of the next one and the next day at school, prepared, organized, I rested, went to bed and slept, and then had coffee upon waking up in the morning.

Chapter 30

In the winter we didn't go out as often as we did in the other seasons. My brother was at the house all the time. His health problems continued. They must have been affected by the seasons. The shorter and colder days in the middle of winter cast a gloominess on him and he otherwise suffered periods of neurosis throughout the year. I had seen him go through some panic attacks and paranoia. I was in the basement more often in the winter. I wore a jacket and pants and sat on the couch under a blanket, and I did schoolwork down there, puzzles in a book, played video games, even all at once, or in the same sitting on the weekend. Going up to the mountain was exciting, it felt homely, as though it was a second home while up there. I hadn't gone since the New Year. Then when February break started, that Friday afternoon we went back up to the mountain.

I first stayed with Will. He and his family had to leave a day early. We ate breakfast in the morning, and then I went over to Alex's condo and stayed with him for the rest of the break. He had invited me earlier that month, and I went over a day sooner.

My parents checked in on me daily. They had used to ski, and they liked to hear how it was. We had adventures on the mountain. My father always asked, "How was your day?"

I replied, "It was good."

That was all I wrote. Alex always laughed. He said, "You can say more than 'It was good.' Maybe tell them something about skiing."

The mountain saw the sunrise first and the sunset last. The snow had some depth and conditions were good. We did not ski every day. Alex did not rush to get out, but we went out in the morning and stayed out all day when the wind was calm. Nick stayed with Layton over break. We met up with them on the mountain every day that we went out. When it snowed, we took long runs and were out all day. And when we stayed in, they came over. Late one evening in the hot tub we saw something in the sky. We had skied all day. Everyone in the hot tub saw a red orb of light floating far off above us. Then it zoomed to the right, then to the left, then it was gone. We argued over what it was. I told them that Ryan and I had seen some kind of aircraft fly over his house as fast as the sound it made traveled when we were playing basketball on his driveway, and then it stopped high in the airspace, it seemed almost as though it was facing us, and then it flew off. At the mountain, the red orb mainly hovered, then fell back behind the treetops. Moments later there were flurries in the air. We planned on getting in a full day the next day.

Most nights we ate dinner at The Bag. We met the other boys and the girls there and we ordered curly French fries and extra house sauce, and then we got desert. Our table talked and laughed and we ordered more drinks. Our waitress then brought the check. We split the bill and put our money together in the middle of the table with a tip and then we went outside after.

Nick and Layton went around the corner to the convenience store. Alex waited outside for them. The girls and I walked through the village. I saw Matt out back behind the lodge on a bench. He was waiting for a shuttle bus. I introduced him to the two gewls. Kristin was not out that night. She may have gone to her house earlier that week. I said, "This is Isabel, and this is Esme. Matt and I play football together."

We had started strength and conditioning after the start of the new year. There was a good chance that I was going to be a running back for the upcoming season. Skiing worked and helped shape my legs. Matt and I lifted weights after school in a gym above the locker room, and so did everyone else on the football team. The room was small and had almost no airflow. They put on fans and played music from the speakers. We exercised for at least an hour. Then we went down to the gymnasium and ran routes. Matt was a quarterback. He was fast and threw the ball well. I ran ins, outs, slants, hooks, posts, flies, and the ball fell right into my hands every time. We practiced at a fast pace, play after play. And if we weren't playing football, it was basketball. We either shot around on the court or played one-on-one or other games for fun. It was always pick-up basketball, but we played all out. It became my favorite sport in the offseason or between seasons.

Matt met the gewls. He said hello to them, but he had to go back to his condo. As he got on the bus, Alex, Nick, and Layton walked down the street and Layton came up to us. "Yessah!" he said. "Eh Mistah, bud. Keep working the magic."

"Get enough Red Bull, Layt?" said Nick.

We thought about what to do for the night. Someone suggested going into the hot tubs. They were right across the street, and we walked across the street and went to the locker rooms. No one bothered to get a change of clothes. At least I did not. I believe we went into the hot tubs in our boxer briefs. The girls must have brought their bathing suits and worn those. On my birthday, the night before the last day of the break, their friend who had an open house invited us to her condo. It filled up fast. Even random kids were there. We played music somewhat softly. At around midnight there was a noise complaint, and everyone ran from the condo. Some people went back to the village to catch a shuttle bus, but the buses had already shut down for the night. Alex and I walked back to his place. In the morning, we went over to the other condo and the girls said that it was fine after everyone left and that the condo was cleaned. Then we got coffee and went and packed our bags and loaded the car. Leaving the mountain was always a bittersweet moment. I had just had my birthday, and it was the end of break. We had skied all week, and I had finished all my schoolwork. When I got to the house, I saw my parents and told them about the trip. My brother was on the couch in the living room. I went down in the basement for the rest of the afternoon.

Chapter 31

The gewls went to a private school. They played some sports, went to events, focused on schoolwork. They had older sisters who were popular, and they were too. A couple weeks after February break, one of their friends from school, Ava, texted me about getting together. She and her friend wanted to drink with me. That reached my heart amid everything else, and I got excited. I supposed that it was the springtime sun beginning to shine brighter and longer. She invited me to her house. We planned to get together that weekend.

In the meantime, I went to school and exercised in the weightroom and in the gym after. Baseball began around that time or a little later that spring. The day that we had planned to get together was on St. Patrick's Day. Some of the other boys went to the mountain for the weekend. I stayed at the house to see Ava. My brother had been feeling better. He drove me to her house, then dropped me off. I got out of the car and Ava met me outside. She brought me into her house and introduced me to her father. I had never met her before. I had not even known of her until earlier that week. But it seemed like she knew me and that we had been acquainted. Like the other girls, or the gewls, she was very pretty. I thought that they must have talked about me and the other boys at their school. Then she brought me outside and led me into her garage, which was separated from her house, and we walked upstairs. The second floor was partially finished and furnished. It kind of reminded me of the basement at my house, but the walls were wood and the ceiling was slanted, unlike the concrete walls and wood rafters in the basement. There was space for storage and plenty of open floor space without furnishing, and it had a bathroom. In the main room, her friend was sitting on the couch.

"Hi," she said. "I'm Anna."

"Hey Anna. I'm Andrew."

"I know."

"I hope you don't mind," said Ava. "She wanted to come over. We all can party!"

"Yes!"

"Woohoo!"

"Ooh, that's nice."

They had peach liqueur and poured a few small glasses. Then we raised our glasses. "Cheers!"

"Cheers!"

We each sipped from our glasses. It was sweet. We were full of energy. The girls had set up a Twister mat on the floor. We went over to it. We did not play a full game, technically, but it got us on the floor. We planted ourselves in a variety of positions on the mat, sometimes stretching across full length. At one point I lay sprawled out on my back. Ava was outgoing. She straddled me. After the game, her boyfriend came upstairs. They went into the bathroom.

Anna and I sat on the couch. She talked about her days at school, at home, on weekends, her time over vacation. New Year's was exciting, but she looked forward to the summer. She liked the ocean and going to the beach. She went shopping sometimes, and she went skiing in the winter too. Then Ava came out of the bathroom.

"Did you give him his present yet?" she asked.

"Not yet." They laughed.

Ava went back in the other room. We leaned in and kissed. She was lustful and passionate, and I was too. We had started on the couch, and after a little while we maneuvered onto the floor.

"Let's have sex."

"Yeah?"

"Yeah."

"Wait, I'm going to give you your present."

She went down on me. I melted. We were on the floor, and I was the wood. The room was dark. It seemed like night, but I saw her. I closed my eyes. I saw stars.

Ava came into the room, and we went into the other room and continued. It was hard to tell how long we were in the other room. My phone was back by the couch. Ava's mother checked on us at some point in the afternoon. We only heard her through the walls.

The next time she came up, there was a car in the driveway, and it had been waiting for a couple of minutes. I had asked my brother to pick me up at five o'clock. More time had passed than expected. Anna and I kissed and hugged and then went into the main room. I got my jacket and phone. We said goodbye to each other and hugged again. I went outside and got in the car. My brother and I drove back to the house. I thought of Ava and Anna, Isabel and Esme, the gewls. My abdomen felt relaxed, light and open. I had dreams of them, and then I woke in the morning refreshed.

Chapter 32

Come Monday, before the school day started, somehow Nick already knew about my date at Ava's house. We sat in the cafeteria and drank coffee. "How was it?"

"It was fun."

"I mean, how did it feel?"

"Really good," I said.

Anna was tan. She had wavy black hair down past her shoulders. Her legs were toned. She played soccer. All day I drew in my notebooks. I did the assigned work for the following day in class and in study hall. I had ideas. I sketched them on the page. I felt pacified. Caught up on work, I got ahead that day, and then at the house I digressed at night and talked to the girls. We planned to get together again over the coming weekend.

I stayed busy all day during the week, I hung out with the boys on the weekends, either at the mountain or in town, went to the gym, played basketball, practiced football and baseball. Irritability within my digestive system had begun to become more apparent in middle school, as my brother's stress and panic exacerbated, and it was most perceptible not after eating or drinking anything, but while wearing elastic waist pants, tight clothing, chewing gum. That was baseball, and part of that was football. Even though changing clothes alleviated some of the abdominal pain, it persisted afterward and long after chewing gum. So, I stopped chewing gum, but there were other triggers to the abdominal pain and irritability. It was milder at times then than it was at others, but difficult to discern them all. I bore those burdens well.

On Friday night I went to Will's house. Charles and the other Will who I skied with were there too. I planned to go over to Ava's house with Anna the next day. We had been texting earlier in the day. I was excited. I told both Wills and Charles about our plan to get together. They liked that. We played games upstairs, basketball with a miniature ball and hoop, knee hockey, possibly hide-and-seek. We were active and ran around the game room.

Eventually we went outside. There was an ice rink in his backyard. He planned to take the rink down the following week or two. It was the beginning of spring, but we skated on it that night. Will played hockey for the school. He was good. The other Will and Charles and I were only starting to play pond hockey. There were a few public spots nearby. Some were rinks, and others were actual ponds. We occasionally went to them that year, but we went more often the following years in high school, and to basketball courts too.

We played two on two. Will and I played against Will and Charles. I was fast on skates and was working on my slapshot, but in the hockey games we played, speed and agility on skates and puck handling were most important. We played with no goalie, and the goals themselves were two-by-fours nailed together in the shape of a rectangle. Its front end had two openings on either side wide enough for a puck to slide through. When it did, that was a goal. The fastest skaters usually scored the most, but they had to know how to handle their hockey stick and the puck while skating around the rink, or else the other team poked the puck away. Our game went back and forth, up one end of the rink and down the other. It was easier to defend the goal than it was to score one. We played full contact. There were some good plays. Will shot and the puck thudded against the front of the goal and slid off. I swept in. I cradled the puck and passed it up the rink to Will. He juked around Charles and led the puck very lightly to the goal, then scored.

That was how the game ended. But we continued to skate under the lights. And the brightest light was in the sky, the moon. The night before, it had been a new moon, and its motion across the meridian left only a crescent celestial body in the sky then. Its light was bright, at least enough for us to buzz around the ice rink and see each other and the puck and the goals.

When we went inside, there were pizza boxes in the kitchen. We each had a few slices. We drank hot chocolate and ate, then went upstairs. Ava's mother texted me. The girls were in the hospital. They had passed out on the second floor of Ava's garage. She didn't mention anything else, only she knew that we were planning to get together tomorrow, that they were both looking forward to it, and that I could see them later, but the playdate had to be postponed.

I was deeply moved by this. I had been looking forward to seeing them. Both Wills and Charles could tell that I was upset, even pained. I said that the girls had gone to the hospital after passing out in their garage upstairs.

"Maybe there was a car left on."

"They could have passed out from the carbon monoxide gas."

Then I thought of that morning, my brother, the tv left on, the dark garage and the car, him rushing upstairs, then me going to school. I remembered that night, that distress, then the newly perceived abdominal pain. I was calm. It was only a play date, but it was much more than that.

Chapter 33

It seemed like the medications that my brother had been administered and was taking were more detrimental to his health than they may have aided him. Some were heavy and had powerful neurological effects and side effects to his body. The process of trial and error with those continued. I went into the house on a Sunday that spring and there was a note on the counter. He was at the hospital and my parents were there with him. I went about my day regularly, finishing assignments, reading, drawing. Even though I had the house to myself, I still went down in the basement.

I made plans with my friends for the coming week. I hung out with Matt more often, almost always after school in the gym. We threw his football and ran routes and played basketball. At the end of the ski season, he invited me to his condo at Sugarloaf for the weekend. It was located right next to a trail and a chairlift. We skied wearing shorts and no shirts with our friend George. The sun felt good. It was getting stronger, and the daylight hours were getting longer. All of us skied wearing light clothing on mild, sunny days more often in subsequent ski seasons, but it was our last weekend at the mountain that year. The last big weekend was dedicated to reggae. It was a festival. We were not at the mountain that weekend, but we celebrated anyway. We kept in touch with the girls, and then we all met up in town one night. In the center of it were many stores and outlets. Everything was within walking distance. Matt and I were dropped off in the center and then met up with Isabel and Esme and Kristin, and then all of us walked around. We ate ice cream and saw a movie. After that, we went to a big store with a giant winter boot out front beside the main entrance. It was a monument, the giant boot, replicating the company's famous footwear. We went inside the store. There was a fish tank along the wall. Toward one end was a small open space underneath that went up inside the tank, and from the outside it appeared to be a hemisphere of air. I went under and in the bubble. I came up essentially in the aquarium. Only my head fit in the bubble. I saw all around the inside of it. Fish swam back and forth and roamed between rock features and aquatic plants. I could see through to the outside, and the others looked like they were underwater. They went in the aquarium next.

We went up a flight of stairs and sat in the lounge area. It had couches and chairs and a grand stone fireplace. The walls were decorated with animal trophies, moose, deer, elk, ox, and on the ground stood a bear. I figured that the girls had already talked to Ava and Anna, but they didn't mention anything. Kristin was a comedienne. We were all looking at the animals. Then suddenly she called me a beast. Isabel and Esme laughed.

We waited on the couches in the lounge for our ride to pick us up. It was Esme's sister. We all fit inside her car. She drove down the road and said, "My nine months aren't up!" Then she turned the music louder.

"I love you, Sophie!"

The next day Matt and I played basketball. Every other day since spring sports had started it was baseball. I was on the freshman team. So was every other freshman except for Will. He made the junior varsity team and pitched and played first base. I still pitched but saw the most action on the mound in the summer league when we had games, double-headers, and tournaments often. He had played in another summer league that traveled frequently and focused on pitching then. We practiced at spots outside the high school and even in the gym when the field was occupied. I ran into my old baseball coach before practice.

"Hey, good to see you."

"How's the best third basemen I've ever had doing?"

"I'm in the outfield now."

"Don't tell me Charles is playing third base."

"Yes."

His father was on the boosters. I stood attentive in the outfield, flit around and made plays when the ball came my way. We won many games. Our season was relaxed, but it went by fast. We did not have playoffs or championships that year, We played on the field for only about a month and a half, and our excitement grew as the summer approached.

Chapter 34

My brother graduated high school in the spring. My parents and I went to the ceremony. It was inside the gymnasium. Matt was there too. I sat beside him. Everyone had to sit on bleacher seats. It was hot and unairconditioned, and the old gymnasium was overflowing with guests. That was an exciting moment for him and for my parents when he graduated, and it was for me too. I went outside after the ceremony concluded.

Summer started early for the seniors. The rest of us still had a couple weeks left to the schoolyear. Preseason football started after that, and then we continued to lift weights, strengthen, and condition at the track two days a week. I was set to be a running back. Every Thursday we had seven-on-seven games at our rival's high school. The players who held the ball on offense went to the games, the quarterback, running backs, wide receivers, and the center. I tweaked my knee in the offseason running a simple route. A part of my knee joint was injured. But I went on conditioning, practicing and playing. With knee injuries, they're not always noticeable. Some are playable. That one happened, and it stung, it pinched. I felt it inside my knee joint. I finished the play strong and the rest after that. I played all season with a sore knee. Most of the time it felt all right, and it hardly affected anything. But now and then, when I stepped down the wrong way, there was sharp pain. Later when I skied on it that coming winter there was more pain. It became weaker from all the exercise, the wear and tear, the high-impact activity. My injuries were all similar in a way. I endured them. Sometimes they healed on their own, and sometimes they did not.

Alex invited me to his house in the middle of the week. I went over after practice. Nick was there. I tripped and hit my left foot against the stairs going up the staircase to his game room. My big toe felt broken. We watched TV, played card games and video games. I had to limp because it was hard to walk. Yet later in the night we went outside and walked through the woods behind his house. They had energy and wanted some fresh air. My whole foot hurt. I stood on one leg and raised my foot. My knee and toe injuries were on the same leg, my left leg, and I limped, lightly pressing down with each step that my left foot took. We went back to the house.

It was around midnight when we got up to the game room. We turned on the tv and then slept.

Alex had a pool in his backyard. We went out there after breakfast. We were either in the water or on the pool deck all day. It was the first private pool that I had been to with a water slide. It curved down from a platform and out over the water. I went down the slide or off the diving board. I had a seven-on-seven football game that night and I counted down the hours by half all morning. My toe had a hard time moving. It was stiff and sort of swollen. I figured that my knee might be more vulnerable. I planned to play hard. Then two girls came over. They had walked across town, and they even brought a pizza. We all sat in the sun in chairs by the water and ate. Afterward they said that they were bloated. They had to wait an hour after eating to swim and sat in chairs and reclined, facing up toward the sky. I lay on a floaty through the afternoon.

Despite the pain in my leg, I played throughout the game that night. I ran routes and had some receptions. We never kept score. Those games were like some practices but without wearing all the gear and running sprints. About half the team stayed behind at the track and conditioned as we played seven on seven. I was on the junior varsity team that year. I was an underclassman. One of my teammates who was a senior brought me home after the game. He cruised in his truck as the sun shone low over the fields.

Later that night, I elevated my leg and laid a pack of ice over my foot and my knee. I sat on the sofa in the basement. The floor and the walls behind boxes and under old toys were concrete. My good old purple dinosaur lay in a bin. Beside it sat other smaller stuffed animals. There was baseball gear, winter jackets and clothing, weights, kitchenware, and boxes. Then the furnace turned on. It rumbled like an engine. That was the basement. It was the beginning of July. I leaned back on the sofa.

Chapter 35

On the Fourth of July I took a ferry to Peaks Island. The island was a popular spot to celebrate the holiday or go on vacation. I met up with Nick on the pier. We walked along the street. Some of his relatives were renting a house on the island. They invited him and a friend or two of his to stay with them for the night. Nick's uncle was my assistant football coach, and he was renting the house. It was up a hill a little way from the oceanfront. We left some supplies for the holiday and celebration beside the house. We had sparklers, water bottles and beer for the night out, celebrating on the rocks and beach.

Then we went into the house. I put my overnight bag on a bed upstairs, and then we went back outside. I wanted to explore the island. The ocean had glistened under the blue sky and sun and the boat coasted through the choppy waters on the way over. It was morning still, and the day was gorgeous. We started down the street, then went down a hill. We walked along a road that hugged the coastline. I saw all the coves, the rocky beaches, the bedrock ledges, and the vast body of water, with little forelands on either side of the view. Waves rolled in and crashed. I picked up a flat rock and threw it sidearm. It skipped along the water, then went into a wave. I had skipped rocks along the surface of the water often in childhood while at the ocean, and that was usually at my grandparents' cottage. I even searched under seaweed for crabs. I found a few. I held them. Then we walked on.

We made it to the other side of the island and went down a road that cut through a wooded area. I heard the crunching of leaves. I looked around. A deer was walking through the woods parallel to us.

"How did that animal make it out to the island?"

"Well. It may have swum."

"Or the planet parted the water."

We came out at a clearing. There was a structure made of concrete at one end of it and it had a wide tunnel that went straight to the other side of the clearing. Shrubs and trees grew on top. The structure was either built underneath and through a hill, or over time plants grew around it and atop and filled in the niches and rounded out the flat surfaces. We went inside, then came out at the other end. We walked back to the house and went inside. His uncle was reading a book at the table. I went upstairs and packed my bathing suit and a towel into a plastic bag, then went downstairs.

"Hey, coach," I said.

"T. Gasser, go!"

I ran out of the house. Gassers were a kind of sprint that we did at practices and for conditioning. We had to sprint down the field and then back. They almost always happened at the end of practice or before practice started if someone had slacked off or made an error. Sometimes it was for little things. Even if our kicker missed a field goal at practice, we all got on the line and had to run. Our coach yelled, "Come on!" And then, "Gasser, go!" When we returned, our kicker went out to try again. Finley got into position. The ball was snapped, placed, and he kicked it through the field goal. The ball rocketed onto the other field. "We need that every time. All right, let's go." Practice ended. It was getting late.

Nick met up with me outside. We walked back to the main pier.

"Check this out," he said. He ran down the pier and then jumped and spun around once before going into water.

"Bravo," I said. "How's the water?"

I stood looking out at the bay. There were a few small islands and on one stood an actual fort. The water was blue and green under streaks of light. The city shone in the distance. I flipped in the air. I dove into the water. It was stimulating to my mind and midsection. I quickly swam to the ladder. I climbed up the pier and dried off with my towel. A few kids showed up and jumped into the water many times. They did not stop and bother to dry off but kept going off the pier and into the water, sometimes doing tricks.

Nick and I got ice cream. We ate dinner with everyone later. It was somewhere outside on the eastern end of the island. We had fish tacos and ceviche by the ocean. We then went back to the house and got our beverages. It was nearing dusk. Soon the sun set over the bay and beyond the city. We found a spot and sat down by the pier, but not on it. The pier had already crowded and filled. People stood around everywhere along the oceanfront. We both opened a can and cheered as the first firework went off and lit the sky. And then more fireworks went off in clusters, some arching down and sizzling like pattering rain. The display took place across the bay on the promenade. We had the best view. Not only did each firework light up the sky but also the water below between our spot and the island ahead, blending silkily into the reflection of the moon almost like the sunset had.

After the display ended, we went down the street with a group of older kids. They led us down a small path and then along a rocky beach to one of the hidden coves. There was a bonfire, and many people stood around it. A group of girls walked up to us. I thought at first that it was Isabel and Ashley and a few of their friends. But it was their older sisters, Emma and Sophie, with a few of their friends. They handed me a beverage. Then Emma hugged me. "You're Andrew."

"Yes."

"Andrew!" said Sophie. "My sister likes you."

We celebrated into the night. The cove had smooth rocks between bedrock and sand, and some flat ones were stacked and formed into cairns. Waves rolled ashore in the moonlight. Most kids stayed overnight on the island. Sparklers glittered on and off, and someone popped a champagne bottle.

The island house was empty in the morning. Coach was outside somewhere on the island. I washed my face and brushed my teeth. Then I walked to the pier and boarded the next ferry. We cruised back to the mainland. I got off the boat and went to a diner down the street. I sat at the bar. The waitress served me coffee. I drank it. She asked, "Would you like more, honey?"

"Yes, please."

Chapter 36

Every sport in the fall had double sessions, one practice in the morning and another at night for two weeks. We called them doubles. Football may have been the toughest out of all the fall sports. We had to wear gear, pads, helmets. Our bodies were knocked around and we hit the ground and got up. The doubles sessions went on for three hours each. Actually, there was a progression to the sessions. The first two days, sessions were two hours long, and we only wore helmets. The following two days, they were two and a half hours long, and we wore shoulder pads, helmets, and shorts. After that, we wore all the gear, shoulder pads, helmets, padded pants, and the toughness began.

In the beginning I was exhausted and sore all day, especially my knee and my toe. I just went through the motions. We ran I don't know how many sprints. Every session, in that case, was the same. Even while sleeping, I dreamt, "Gasser, go!" "Gasser, go!" I was not in breast at practice for the first week. Then, one day at a time, everything became a bit easier. The intensity was the same, but I had become somewhat acclimated to all the exertion, physical and mental. The last day of doubles was almost sad. Not because it was the end of the preseason. But really because it was the end of summer.

The first game was on Monday. School started the following week. Matt and I made plans to hangout. In a way we wanted to celebrate all the hard work, the end of the preseason, and more to come. On Sunday afternoon we got a ride downtown. We walked through the Old Port. The sun was out, streets were busy. We were hungry. We ordered hamburgers and French fries. I ate a lot that afternoon. Doubles had just ended, and it seemed like a reward for all that work and effort. So, we ate well. We each had a hamburger, two buns and two patties, a cup of fries, and more fries in the bag.

We finished everything, then filled our cups with peanuts and left the restaurant.

Outside I brought Matt down a wharf. We sat on a bench overlooking the water, sailboats in the bay. Some were moored. Many were out for a sail. Seabirds flew overhead. A few landed and waddled toward our bench. Pigeons flit around. We ate the peanuts, then tossed the shells into the water.

"I like downtown," said Matt.

"Yeah."

"There's a lot to do. Dates to museums and restaurants. And there's a lot of art."

"Not, what art these nuts. But more like, *what is anything?*"

Matt finished eating his peanuts. I had several left. Peanuts are high fodmap. I dumped the rest onto the ground and threw the bag away. The seabirds came over and poked at the shells with their beaks. We walked up the hill toward city center and along the way I smelled a smorgasbord. Then we walked by all the bars and lounges. The upscale ones allured me the most.

We walked along Congress. We went by the Longfellow house. Earlier that summer, before preseason, Ben, Miles, Ryan, and I had gone inside and went through the museum. Then we sat on a bench in the garden out back. The grounds were well-kept. There were plants, pathways, butterflies. Matt and I went further down Congress and looped around the Museum of Art. We did not go inside but kept walking, then at the end of the street, we stopped at a cafe. It was Taiwanese. We sat at a booth. Isabel and Esme met us there. We all ordered food and drinks at the counter. Our bubble tea came out first. The girls brought a water bottle. We drank our tea and laughed between bubbles, just as the sweet woman who owned the cafe called the rest of our order.

"Noses," said Matt.

Both girls were quick. Matt touched his nose first. I touched mine last. I had a sip of tea and then went and got our food. Bao buns for everyone. They were steaming hot, delicious. We ate them, and I was surprised to have eaten as much as I had.

Isabel lived down the block and around the corner. We all went to her apartment after leaving the café. It was nice inside, and cozy.

The building was old, yet the apartment seemed new. Isabel and her mom and her sister lived there. I imagined living with them.

We had the living room to ourselves. We sat in a circle. We talked and laughed. Then Matt said, "We have a game tomorrow…"

Yet a bottle half full of spirits was passed around. We sipped from it. Maybe we played spin the bottle with it. Music came on. We were possibly getting out of control but having a good time. My joints, muscles, sores that had been aching all day then seemingly faded. I danced. I did not have rhythm, but I moved. The girls liked it and patted my glutes. Matt was playing on a piano. We went on for hours. Minutes began to blur together. Her sister was in her room. I was in the living room, and she was down the hall. "Emma!" The apartment had a Victorian interior. Notes echoed and drifted outside into the night air.

Then early in the morning, I woke in the basement at the house. The lights were on. I went upstairs to my bedroom. Some of the food from yesterday afternoon was on the floor next to my bed. My parents were still asleep. I did not recall going back to the house. I only remembered eating in the afternoon, meeting up with the girls, the rustic wood floors, Matt playing the piano, dancing, getting a ride from an older girl. I got paper towels from the kitchen and soap from the laundry. I had lifting for football at 7:30 a.m.

I opened the windows, turned on the fan, watched the sunrise. I felt better but tired. I walked downstairs. My parents were sitting at the table. "Are you ready for your game today?"

"Yes," I said. "And I need to leave for lifting. Can you give me a ride?"

"Yes, of course."

"Make sure to eat before you go."

My head ached in the weight room. The world spun. I bench-pressed and squatted. I thought, I have a game in five hours, and we're lifting before? How am I doing this? Then I pressed through it. I finished the workout and went straight to the house. I lay in bed and rested.

The game that afternoon was away. We warmed up by stretching and doing calisthenics and running plays. Matt and I went over to the water bucket. The day before had been good. Were we ready for our game? "Yes!"

Our team kicked off first. We went back and forth with the other team. At the end of the first quarter the score was nil-nil. Alex, our fullback, scored the first touchdown. He and I were linebackers on defense. The other team liked to run the ball up the middle. We filled the gaps and contained the outsides. One of their running backs ran almost headfirst with the ball. He dove through the linemen and his helmet went into my stomach. We went down. I rubbed my stomach.

On offense our team used the triple-option formation. There were five linemen, two wide receivers, two wingbacks, a fullback, and a quarterback. On second down, Matt kept the ball and went for a long fast run along the sideline. Their safety tackled him twenty yards before the endzone. Matt was our quarterback. He got us the first down. We ran the same play but to the other side and I went in motion. He called the cadence. The ball was snapped. He faked the handoff to Alex, then swept around to the outside. I ran a stride or two behind him. Then, at the line of scrimmage, he pitched the ball back to me. I caught it and ran further to the outside and went past their cornerback. Then their safety. Then I crossed the goal line. I scored my first touchdown!

I jogged off the field. I took my helmet off and went to the water bucket. We won the game. We were good. We did not let up touchdowns often and scored almost every time we had the ball. All the conditioning throughout the school year and then the summer, the doubles, the sprints, and the lifting went into that. And the night before a game day!

We took a knee ln the sideline. Our coach went over the game, the performance, and we all got snacks. I needed some ice and elevation. I went back to the house and down to the basement and went on my game console. I read and drew, and I recharged for the next practice and for the schoolyear to start.

Chapter 37

I began having friends over sometimes on the weekend. We sat around in the basement. That was when it became referred to as the basement. We played games, relaxed, and once or twice, tried to party. We had music, disco balls, strobe lights. Miles and I had girls over a couple of times, but mostly it was the boys. That lasted for only the beginning of that schoolyear and a bit over the summer and at the end of the previous year, and then it became the basement again later in high school. My brother went to the hospital for more anxiety and panic attacks. He sat in the living room when I got home from practice. I always poured a glass of water in the kitchen and then went upstairs to shower and change clothes. We had a long preseason, and the regular season went by fast. It was about two months long. Our varsity team was knocked out in the second round of playoffs. I played in every game on kickoff and kick return all season, and I went in on offense and defense toward the end of some games when we were ahead. Most juniors and seniors played on varsity. The following season I planned to play all game. My grandparents had gone to watch some of the games. They came over to the house for Thanksgiving, along with a few other relatives, and then again on Christmas. I had eggnog with Papa. He was 92 years old. He fell asleep on the chair early in the afternoon, then right before we had dessert, he woke up. We ate cake and pie and ice cream, and he ate many assorted Italian cookies too. Nana drank a cup of tea. Then after everyone left that night, I met up with Ryan and Ben, and Ben had gotten his driver's license earlier that year. We tried to figure out something to do. We sat in the parking lot in his car for a little while.

"Merry Christmas," said Ben.

"T, when are you going to the mountain?"

"Tomorrow," I said.

This time I stayed with Matt, and so did Nick. On the first night at the mountain, we went out to eat at a restaurant. We sat at a booth and ate dinner, then saw if any other kids were at the mountain and in the village area. No one else was up yet. We went back to the condo, watched TV, and then got some rest.

In the morning, we woke up early. I drank a cup of coffee. It was overcast outside. We ate breakfast at the table by a window and faced the front of the mountain, the trail arteries, and the summit. Behind us I heard the trickle of coffee filling a coffee mug. We relaxed for a moment longer, and then we put on our ski gear and left the condo.

Each run stimulated my mind and perhaps they did for the others too. The cool air blew through us along the trails going down to the chairlift. My body loosened up and coordination fully activated, and my mind continued in momentum after slowing down at the bottom. Matt and I sometimes had interminable discussions on intellect. He liked science and math. I did too, and philosophy. Then we got off the lift ready for the run.

"A star dies and becomes a black hole. You could see the star but then you couldn't see anything. Where are you?"

The three of us went all around the mountain that morning. The conditions were icy. But after a snowstorm, and more so during one, they were prime. We went back to the condo for lunch, then went outside again. We skied until the lifts closed that day. I had brought hand warmers and wore them in my gloves. We wanted to ski for a full day before calling it a day.

That evening we went to the gym to play basketball and there we met Layton. The four of us tried playing two on two, but then Layton and Nick went upstairs. Matt and I continued playing one on one. We checked the ball behind the three-point line. He crossed over and drove to the hoop for a layup. I had stayed on him as he leapt up and rolled the ball past my hand and off the backboard into the hoop. We went and checked again behind the three-point line. I stripped the ball and cleared it. I pulled up to the elbow and shot the ball and scored. My skills had developed. Some days I scored almost every time I had the ball. Most of my points came from shooting the ball as opposed to laying the ball up and into the hoop. I went all around the basketball court. I drove to the hoop, stepped back, faded and shot the ball, and then I scored again. When there were teams, I moved around the perimeter of the three-point line and shot the ball when I was open. While practicing, I rarely missed. And while playing in games, I missed sometimes and that was when my stroke was off, but I had a good three-point percentage.

Our one-on-one game went down to the end. Layton and Nick watched from the second floor. We checked the ball at the top of the court. I passed the ball to Matt, and he passed it back to me, starting the possession. I thought quickly, then I drove to the hoop and looped around to the low post. I set myself and pumped the ball but held onto it. Matt went for the block and jumped past me. I shot the ball wide open and scored. Next possession, I missed the basket, and the ball went out of bounds. We checked the ball at the top of the court. Matt faked the three-point shot. I lunged forward, turned, and then stayed with him as he broke away for the hoop and did a reverse layup and scored. It was smooth. I got the ball back. We checked, and right away, I shot the ball. It was far behind the three-point line. It almost seemed like the ball came out of my hands from more of a push rather than a flick. We watched the ball arch through the air, the seams spin, and still, it went into the hoop and nearly swished the net.

"Ay!" hollered Layton and Nick.

That was it. The game finished, and then we called a shuttle. We went up to the village and walked around. It was cold outside. Four days later, on New Year's Eve, it was frigid. We watched the fireworks. Our friend Max invited us to someone's condo, and we went there afterward. They invited us and some others too. It was near the bottom of the trail that went the furthest down the mountain. The slope of the trail was almost level from top to bottom. I walked on the trail with Isabel and Esme. The night sky showed clear above the treetops between the gaps in the clouds, and a few stars swept across the same gaps along respective paths in outer space.

We made it to the bottom of the trail and went to the condo. A couple of people were standing outside. We walked past them and went inside and climbed the stairs. There was a room with a ping pong table and games and another with a couch and some chairs. A group of people were playing pong. Layton and Nick were already there, and they had called the next game. Matt was in the other room. Music was on. Many people were there. Then it got louder. Some people were obnoxious. I went into the other room. Nick saw me.

"Andrew," he said. "I need help with something."

"What is it?"

"I can't find Layton and we're playing pong next."

"He's probably around. Let's check the other room."

There was a crowd of people. They began counting down from ten, nine, eight, seven… all the way to three, two, one, and then the clock struck midnight. Everyone cheered, kissed, or raised a glass. The celebration continued and even heightened a bit in noise and cheer until the fire alarms went off. We rushed outside, and laying on a snowbank at the edge of the pavement was Layton.

"You okay, bub?" said Nick.

He groaned. We helped him up to his feet and then called for a shuttle bus and waited under the stars with the girls. The bus pulled up to the curb and we all got on. Inside it was completely full. Every seat was taken and some people stood in the aisle. We almost had to yell to each other. The radio was on and suddenly it got louder. People up front started singing a Fleetwood Mac song. Then everyone started singing. And then someone shouted, "Fleetwood Mac at the lodge!" People cheered. The noise grew as the sing-along went on and the bus rode up to the village.

If the band was in fact at the lodge, we did not see them play. Those venues were usually 21 and over, and nothing else was open. We all went back to the condos. I made waffles for Matt and Nick, and then we all went to bed.

Chapter 38

We skied mostly in the woods. The groomed trails had a snow depth of several feet, but throughout the day, they all got skied off and their surfaces became hardpacked and icy. A lot of the glades had a top layer of fluffed snow in some parts, and most of the wooded areas were otherwise soft. We stuck to those areas. My knee felt painful at times, when it flexed too far, hyperextended, and when I crouched down. It snowed one day in the middle of the week. The trails we went on were empty, and lines were fast. We tried to ski all day. Almost every run we went through the woods. The glades were dense. We wove through the trees gliding over the soft snow. The section of the mountain that we were on was new. A couple years earlier, the ski resort expanded, and hundreds of acres of new terrain opened off to the side of the mountain between the main peak and another peak. After going through the new terrain one run, we missed the junction of trails where most people came out of the woods at the bottom of the chairlift, but we went further and further down the mountain. There were traces of some light but discernible tracks that had been covered in a layer of snow that we followed. Trees went from hardy evergreens at the top of the new terrain, right around where the tree line stopped, to mostly birch further down the basin. We traversed along some flatlands and used our poles to push ourselves along. Many sections briefly went uphill. I began heating up under my gear, and energy diffused from my body into the atmosphere. After pushing nonstop for a while, we found a trail. We got on at the bottom of it, right along where we had walked to celebrate New Year's Eve. It was the foot of the mountain. And there was a chairlift. We got on.

The entrance to the woods was hidden. It was up there, toward the top of the mountain, which seemed like a beast. We were three lift rides away from the top. We slowly made our way. Once there, we cut over to the woods. We stayed in bounds. There were a few spots that were normally steep and icy and sometimes bare. I glided over them, as though they were clouds. The others stopped before a cliff. I went around the outside. My knee hurt already. I waited for them. Layton went first. He practically floated for a moment and his arms windmilled. He landed crouched and stopped and the top layer of snow clouded the air. We waited off to the side. Matt went, and he stayed composed through the landing. He came over. I bumped his fist. Nick went next. He skied off the cliff and hit the ground and fell back. He got his poles and stood up and then skied down to us.

"Aw."

"How was that?"

"I need some back medicine," he said.

I thought, for my knee, *that sounds nice*. And then we skied exceptionally well, gracefully even. My mind synced with the moment and every movement felt connected.

Going up the mountain someone asked, "What time is it?" And then toward the top, "Huh, it's only been three minutes."

Later, we ate a quick lunch. But even that seemed to last longer than it did. We recharged and then went outside. We stepped into our skis and pushed and swayed to the chairlift and got on, then grouped together at the top.

Every run thereafter that day cruised along. I went with the motion of the wind and felt a sense of control. It had been a full week. I was planning to go back to the house a little early to celebrate the February birthdays with my family, my brother's and mine. Then in the middle of the week my parents called me.

"Your brother's in the hospital."

"No, really?"

"Yes, you can stay at the mountain for the rest of the week. Celebrate your birthday up there this time."

"Okay."

That was all. I stayed at the mountain until the end of the week. We went out to dinner with a group of friends the day that we were going to have a big dinner at the house.

A few weekends later was St. Patrick's Day, and I remembered the previous year, then smiled, recalling that it was good. We went to a party at a condo the night before. When we skied, we wore only shorts and sunglasses, socks and ski boots, but no gloves or jackets. I skied wearing earbuds and listened to music on low that mixed with the woosh of the air going down the mountain. One gets into a rhythm. My knee felt fine. I went slowly on the flatter parts and kind of danced. Isabel and Esme patted my glutes going by. Springtime glowed around.

Nick and I stayed at a condo on the last weekend of our ski season. It had an indoor hot tub in a sunroom with pots and plants located beside the entryway. We went out in the morning and again wore shorts. By the afternoon, my knee and his back were in fact sore. We walked to The Bag for dinner.

There was a wait. We sat off to the side quietly, attuned to the noises, the clinks, steps, croaks and groans, and everything blended harmoniously. My lens blurred in the peripheral, but in the center, it gleamed with the light. We sat at a table and drank water and each ordered a few different items on the menu. The table was full. I ate everything. My knee no longer ached. We paid and then went outside. We walked down the trail to the lounge. There were couches and chairs and a big fireplace. The tv was on, playing a basketball game. We watched that for a moment.

Then Nick said, "I can't find my key."

I raised my eyebrows. We got up, looked around. We searched on the floor, under the couch, and the chairs, then went outside. We walked up the trail and focused attentively on the ground. We both turned on our flashlights and a couple of times thought that we spotted his key, but they were only leaves resting on top of the snow. We went inside the restaurant and looked around the booth that we had sat at, but it was not there. Back down the trail, we again did not see it along our path. We stopped about halfway down. I was anxious to get back to the condo. "Did you check all your pockets?" I asked.

He checked again. "Yeah."

Then, "Well uh—"

"Hold on. What's that?" I shone my light on the ground. And there on the trail, right on top of the snow, was the key. We walked back to the condo. We changed for bed and then went to sleep.

Chapter 39

Earlier that year Nick had invited me to Florida over our vacation in April. His family knew the owner of a leading sporting goods company, Under Armor, who owned a house on Sanibel Island at which we were going to stay. Excitement grew throughout the week from the previous weekend when we had skied to that Friday, in the morning, the afternoon, and then the night.

My father drove me to the airport in the morning. Departure time was at 6:00 a.m. Nick and his parents flew out from a different airport at the same time. I arrived ahead of schedule and waited in the terminal for a moment in front of my gate, then walked around. It was a small airport, and it must have been around 5:00 a.m. I bought a coffee and then went back to my seat. To my surprise, sitting across the aisle was one of my teachers. We said hello to each other. We were both going to Florida.

My flight was called. I boarded the plane and sat beside the window and began to listen to jazz music. The plane took off, and as we rose in altitude and peaked and continued flying south, I watched the sky turn from all dark to mostly dark with a little streak of orange along the horizon, and that little streak of light grew until the sun came into sight and the morning sky lit up. Then we flew above clouds. They looked like oceans of snow. I enjoyed some of the views on airplane rides, and that weightless feeling you can get at takeoff.

We were on schedule to land in Washington D.C. Then as we neared the airport, we flew directly into the thick grey clouds of a storm. The visibility was low, but I thought that I saw lightning form. There was turbulence. People began to fret. Someone on the intercom announced that it was not possible to land in Washington D.C. Then our pilot turned the plane around. Maybe twenty minutes later we landed in Baltimore.

The soonest connecting flight was scheduled to depart six hours later. I walked around the airport, went outside, then back in. I found my gate and sat down.

Later I went to a restaurant around the corner and sat at the bar and ordered a hamburger for lunch. I drank water, and after eating, I had a coffee. I watched TV, I yawned a couple times into my hand. I paid and then left the restaurant and found an empty seat outside of my gate and took a nap.

At around 7:00 p.m. we arrived in Fort Myers. I waited inside the airport for a couple hours. Nick and his parents also experienced some delays with their flight. It was the same as my flight, because of the strong winds and thunderstorms. They first landed in Tampa, then drove to Fort Myers. I met them outside. We drove to the island with the windows down. We crossed over the waterway and went down the road a little way and then arrived at the house.

I was in awe. The place was magnificent. It had a white exterior and a small front yard with trees growing above the rooftop on either side, and inside there were large windows overlooking the water, carpeted and tile floors, and a small elevator spanned each floor of the house. Outside there was a pool, hot tub, deck, and patio with an oceanfront backyard and beach from which a private pier extended out over the water that had possibly the best fishing on the island.

We woke up early in the morning and went outside. It felt nice, warm and a bit humid. We walked out on the pier. The water had small waves like those in a lake but was otherwise calm, glistening in the sunlight. We got two fishing poles and began to fish and we caught a few little ones right away. I held them, then placed them back in the water. They swam about slowly, glowing in the sunlight going further out into the sea. After a little while we went inside and ate breakfast, then rode bikes along pathways around the island. I tried to climb a tree. There was a coconut in the cluster of fronds up top. I did not quite get up to the coconut. Instead, I picked a good one off the ground beside the tree and held onto it in my knapsack. We went on.

Lunch that afternoon was at Dairy Queen. We went there every day. I finished my meal and had desert. My mouth waters, thinking of the food before digestive distress, ice cream, wheat, spices and the sauce.

We went back to the house and put the bikes away. Out back I dove off the pier and went for a swim. The water was warm. I floated on my back, absorbing the sun, and then I swam to the beach and got a paddleboard. I stepped on and went out a little way into the bay. The bridge connecting the island to the mainland lay out over the bay directly ahead. The other side of the island faced the gulf. Paddleboarding on that side may have been turbulent or become nearly a surf. I went back toward the shore. I lay down flat on the paddleboard in front of the pier. I saw the coastline, beaches and trees, and then I noticed some movement from the other direction. I turned my head and coming toward me was a fin. It was poking out just above the water. I stayed still. My paddleboard gently rocked. It approached me in a swift manner moving above the surface of the water. It was more than just a fish, I realized, and I fell off the paddleboard into the water. It continued swimming and swam tranquilly further down the coast and out of sight. I had heard that dolphins can have an affinity for humans. I got on the paddleboard and thought that it might swim back with a few more dolphins, squirt water in the air, and trill around the pier.

The next day we went on a boat ride around the island. Nick and I drove down the road in a golf cart. The marina was about a quarter mile from the house. We parked, and then we got on the boat and set out on the water. Our tour guide curved around the point. We saw the lighthouse, and we had biked to it earlier, but it seemed more prominent from afar. In the other direction, to the south, was all open water. The boat picked up speed, and we made a big wake. I looked away for a moment as the wind nearly glued me to my seat. Then I looked up, thought this is heaven, the blue sky and sun set high, the rush of air blowing by. And then I looked back, and several dolphins were jumping out of the water from the wake right behind the path of the boat. They arched through the air and dove back into the ocean, so gracefully, then came up on the other side and arched in the air again, so gracefully, so playfully.

They followed the boat to Captiva Island, and then we had to slow down. Our guide looped around to Sanibel. I sat back in my seat on the way to the marina.

Later we went out on the pier to fish. We each cast our lines and reeled them in. I let mine go and it soared through the air straight ahead and went into the water. I reeled slowly, then quickly, then slowly, and then I hooked something. It seemed to be a big fish by the way it moved and pulled with difficult maneuvers. I had only gone fishing a few times before then when I was much younger, deep-sea fishing on a boat thirty miles offshore, but more often from a pier. We caught and kept some of the fish, but most often we caught a type of fish called dogfish that we then let go back into the water. Someone yelled, "Aw, the fish bit me!" Well, the moment the fish was reeled aboard it became no longer the guide's boat, but the fish's boat. And that was one dogfish. There were many more. They were strong, agile fish. They swam and changed directions in the water fast. I thought that the fish that I was reeling in was of the same species. It went left, right, back out to sea. It pulled tight. The line could oscillate, I thought, and resonate notes when strummed.

"Give it some slack. There, just a little."

"All right."

"Aw yeah. There you go."

Thrilled, I broke a sweat. I reeled, it pulled. The fish came closer to the pier. It was practically swimming to me. The water was opaque, but it surfaced. I saw its sleek skin and its big flat head broader than the rest of its body. It was a hammerhead shark. I thought, right on!

I pulled the fish onto the pier. It wriggled like an eel, and even more so when I rubbed its belly. Then two figures walked toward us on the beach. I held up my catch. "Kiss the fish!" I kissed it, and its tail wagged about. Then I unhooked it and set it into the water. It calmly swam around in circles before me. I smiled. The two people walking on the beach almost seemed familiar. Nick and I stood on the pier, looking down at them.

"Hey Adam. Come on up. We're fishing."

We were casual about it. Adam went to our school, and his friend Rory, who was there with him, went to school in the town next door. I had played football against him. They were also staying on the island, just down by the point. They were only a short walk away, and they came back to the pier often to fish. Everyone caught some fish, but that hammerhead was the mightiest catch that week, and the dolphins were the most spectacular.

In the coming days, we spent a lot of time fishing from the pier, mainly because Adam and Rory were always there. On our last night we had dinner in Captiva. The restaurant was on the beach facing the gulf. There were some waves. The water was relaxing. I ate fish tacos and drank from a coconut. The setting dimmed as the sun dipped below the horizon and cast red and orange and yellow light across the sky. We drove back to the house in a convertible and the air rushed by us in our seats like it had on the boat.

I woke early in the morning. I brushed my teeth and got my belongings together. A taxi picked me up at 4:00 a.m. The flight was at 6:00 a.m. I arrived at the airport, boarded the plane. This time we landed and had a layover in Washington D.C. There had been no thunderstorms along the way. I ordered breakfast and a coffee. I waited at the gate, and then the flight was called. We lined up, and standing just a few spots back was Cameron, who went to school with the gewls. He had flown in from the west and had a layover in Washington D.C. too, and on the plane we both had window seats. I looked out to see the sunrise and thought of the sunsets the previous nights and the interconnected world about.

Chapter 40

I had signed up for indoor track in the winter, and I ran after school every day for a few months, mainly to get faster for football, and supposing that my knee will get stronger. Then I ran track in the spring instead of playing baseball for the same reason, to condition, try to get faster for football and strengthen my legs. So, I did track and field with Ben and a few others. He focused on the high jump and triple jump, and I only ran sprints. We both had shin splints. My knee had gotten worse over the winter. Then it developed Osgood-Schlatter's. It was painful only around the front of my knee where the tibia meets the kneecap. Otherwise, the dominant pain in my knee which I had been experiencing all year was inside and behind my knee. We ran every day. It was the same with indoor track except that I ran with Hannah. She was fast, and she had strong toned legs. We warmed up together, stretched, did calisthenics, and ran. She wanted to get me, Ben, Miles, and a few of her friends together for her birthday and rent a hotel room for the night, to play music, games, and dance. The idea was formed on the spot as we ran around the hallways in our school. That was indoor track. For practice, we ran sprints down the long hallways. We could not practice outside on the track like we did in the spring because of the snow. Only once a week we had practice at an indoor track. The whole team took a bus there and back. Hannah and I sat together. At the indoor track we ran openly. It was much less congested than the hallways in our school. No one ran into each other or any open lockers or doors. The practice was shortened to make up for the travel time. After running half as many sprints as usual, practice finished. I got on the bus first, and then after a few other people, Hannah got on. She sat down and the bus pulled out and started driving. We never celebrated her birthday like we had been planning to that year.

I passed my driver's test shortly after the trip to Florida. I drove Maddy home after practice, and Ben sat in the back of the car. Her house was down the road from the school. Hannah and I both drove to the mall over the weekend. We ate frozen yogurt. My car was called the Honda. It was a two-door.

I later drove to the movies and to the beach with Isabel and Esme. We got together more often and met up at restaurants a few times before the schoolyear ended. No one had to figure out or wait on rides. The summer seemed fuller since most of us except for Ryan had started driving. We were more active each day between preseason practices and on the weekends. We still got rides on certain occasions, like to some concerts to which we all got tickets. Ben and Reid and Miles and I went to one over the summer. It was part of Wiz Khalifa's summer tour. Mac Miller and Kendrick Lamar also performed that night. The stage was outside. There had been another concert part of another tour on a wharf the previous year. The current concert was in a big field. There were thousands of chairs set up, and then the chairs were moved aside or stacked into one big pile toward the front. Then people stormed the fence, trying to get as close to the stage as possible. There was a mosh pit and then a fight. We all got split up among the crowd. Miles went off to the side a bit. He found an upright chair and sat down. He enjoyed the music as is. He said that even from his angle the people toward the front seemed wild and funny. I was in that crowd or among them in a more relaxed section. So were Reid and Ben. Later, after finding each other, we saw a few other older kids from our school. That brought me back to those times at the lake in the summer as young kids, all the fireworks, swimming, tubing, kayaking, swinging, and eating by the shore.

The next day we all went to the beach. Our usual spot was at one end of the cove next to the mouth of a river. It was the widest section of beach and seemed to have the softest sand. We laid out on top of our towels for most of the day. We lazed and then went for a leisurely swim but only for a little while. I always tried to go to the beach often in the summer, to unwind or to uplift. When my brother's health condition relapsed and there was distress at the house, the beach was always calming, refreshing and inspiring. And it never changed. Only the tide came in or pulled away. The rest had been there ages ago, and it will be there ages to come, the sun, the sand, the breeze, the trees sprouting up, all blending with the horizon. Development sat back on the land in contrast with the season. The quick trips to the beach in the summer carried my mind's stride. There was no hill, just sun, surf and sand, and skiing in the spring had that, snow and slopes. They transitioned well, those days that seemed like they'll never end.

Chapter 41

The summer wound down fast but gave many full days that gave the season or the vacation a longer duration. Preseason sports began. I played for the varsity football team. I started on offense and defense and played on special teams, kickoff and kickoff return. They wanted to keep me going throughout all of our games. Though my knee injury had exacerbated throughout the previous year, then the summer, and then preseason, I played through it and worked hard as we prepared for the season. I had bulked up and put on weight over the summer. I weighed one hundred and seventy pounds going into the season and maintained agility. Then at the end of doubles, we had an intrasquad scrimmage game. Our coaches must have drafted the teams. The game was a mix between practice and full-on play. Matt and I were on opposing teams. It had gone back and forth all game, practicing, playing, and scoring. His team had possession. He called the cadence. The ball was snapped back to him and he held onto it and ran toward the outside, my side, then cut in and ran up field. I went in to make the tackle. I stepped down and planted my left leg first. We hit at that moment, with my left leg hyperextended, and then we both went down. He got up, but I stayed on the ground. There was pain in my knee. It had popped. I felt it. And I thought that I had heard it as I was making the tackle. I was helped up but could not stand strong on my left leg. I went to the sideline and sat on the bench. Our trainer taped a bag of ice around my knee. I sat out for the rest of the game and by the end of it my knee had swelled a bit.

Two days later our trainer looked at my leg before practice started. The front, back, and both sides of my knee were still swollen, but it seemed like most of the swelling was inside the joint. The outside looked normal. Its range of motion was low. My lower leg felt almost disconnected from my upper leg. Walking was like playing the piano without the sound. It had not taken long to realize that something was wrong with my knee, even the previous season. She told me to sit out that practice and then referred me to an orthopedic doctor.

I went to her office after school the following day. She evaluated my knee, and I performed a few exercises mainly to test my knee's range of motion, its bending and stretching, and its strength. I performed well and said that my knee felt fine. I had in mind the game on Friday night. She said that all the swelling around my knee indicated the likelihood of an injury. Then she referred me to an orthopedic clinic. I scheduled an appointment to get an MRI for the following afternoon.

I went into the machine. No one was with me. I was alone. I thought that the machine was talking to me. "Breathe in… hold your breath… breathe out…" It processed images of my knee inside and out. It saw inside of me, made a few noises, flashed some lights. I blinked, breathed in, breathed out. And then I slid out the other end. I left the clinic and drove to practice. The team trainer called me along the way. She had seen the MRI images already. My ACL was ruptured. My meniscus was torn in three places. I was out for the season. Still, I went to practice. The team was briefed on my injury. I stayed at practice and watched them run around.

The following week I went back to the orthopedic clinic and lay on an operating table, thinking about the previous year, playing through all the discomfort, skiing and running, hyperextending my leg, and playing on it again throughout that summer. I thought that at least one of those meniscal tears had formed the previous season and exacerbated over the course of the year. Yet I had still placed third in states for the 100-meter relay, along with the rest of the relay team. My mind was in stride and then it stopped. I lay still for a while. My surgeon administered the anesthesia. Then he counted down from ten. At eight he seemed like a beautiful man. At seven I began to laugh. At five my eyes closed, and I felt elated. Then I woke up to bright light.

For several days I lay in my bed. Someone from school brought over brownies. I thanked him and asked if he wanted one. But he had to start on his schoolwork. I caught up and got ahead on mine as I recuperated, and that was how my school year started. Between that, the exercises, and rest, I got back into puzzles, online board games, and read and studied extra material. I was even deeper into philosophy, a foundation of theory, founded upon consciousness. And that philosophy really seemed to make the world grand, a continuation of consciousness. In the other world I had gone to school, then practice. Instead in the moment, I exercised body and mind and ate meals in bed. I drank water and rested.

Soon I got up and hopped around on crutches, moving adroitly through the house. On Monday I went to school. Classmates carried my backpack in the halls between classes. I navigated through the crowds. Doors were held open. I pulled out a chair and sat down. Hannah's sister came over to the house with one of her friends. I was recovering from a knee injury, but I walked without crutches. My exercises then were limited to non-weight-bearing, sitting or lying down.

The football season commenced. A few changes were made to the starting lineup, but the team continued to play strong. I went to the games and practices and hopped around on the sideline. All the players were focused at the games. I was alone as they went from drill to drill and ran sprints at practice. Then Alex tore his ACL. It happened during a game. He got surgery and then joined me on the sideline. We watched and cheered. We still went out to the huddle during breaks, the chants, "States on three. One, two, three, states!"

But they lost during the playoffs. However, the soccer team was good. They played in the state championship game. It was three hours away. Will and I went to it in his car. It was my first weekend off the crutches, and my leg sort of stiffened in the seat to the point that my knee felt worse than the actual injury had. But that meant that my knee was healing. Doctors said that it will take another five months for the injury to fully heal. The timeline for anyone recovering from an ACL replacement surgery was six months, but I estimated three to four months for me to recover. I limped at first because my leg was weak. Someone at the game gave me their water bottle. I had a sip and cheered. Ben and Miles played in the game, as a midfielder and a forward, respectively. Neither scored, but they won the game. They were state champions! Some fans jumped the fence and rushed the field. Will said, "Man, I wish I had played soccer."

"You play golf and you're good at it."

"Yeah."

"Win states in baseball."

"Okay."

A few days later, Ben invited me to the University of Vermont. His sister Sarah went there for college, and he wanted to celebrate his victory again after they had celebrated a little on the night of the championship game. We left on Friday after school. It was a long drive. I sat in the back of his car and stretched my leg out on the seat. When we arrived, my knee felt fine. The scar tissue had begun to break up more rapidly once I got off the crutches, but its range of motion was still low, and the joint stiffened rather easily. We went into someone's room. They were having a small pregame. People were playing games. In the middle of the room there was a game of pong.

I called, "Next game."

Ben's sister and I were up. We got behind one end of the table and went back and forth with the other team, arching the ball across the table into the cups arranged in a triangle. A few more people came into the room and watched the game. Sarah shot the ball like someone playing darts. They were down to two cups. We had a few more. I shot the ball and scored. Then she went, and the ball flew straight through the air. It looked good and went in. We won the game.

She and her friends brought us to a party. We walked through the house, then through the neighborhood. We walked to another place and went inside, then another, and maybe one more after. Ben and I were in high school, his sister was an artist, and her friends were cool.

We went back to the dorm room. I had some leg medicine. My knee had a fuller range of motion. That was part of the celebration. It may have been an unusual night for us. Some of her best paintings then were hanging on the wall. One was of an otherworldly woman. "A mi me gusta," I said.

That was all that I recalled in the morning before we had gone to bed. We left the room and walked to a dining hall and ate breakfast, then drove down the road to the center of town. I had been there before with my aunt and uncle. We browsed around some of the shops. I looked at the coffee mugs and other merchandise. Then we walked down the road and stood on an overhang above the water. Ahead was a big lake, and on the other side were the Adirondack Mountains of New York. Above the lake and the land the sun shone. It was autumn, and we had just missed the peak foliage.

Chapter 42

There were fewer extracurricular activities to do for most of that winter because of my knee injury. I could not run track, play hockey outside or basketball in the gym, or any other high-impact activities until completing the recovery. When others played basketball, I still went to the gym. They played as I performed my leg exercises, lifted weights, and shot free throws on the other side of the gym. I wanted the practice and play but couldn't do the high-impact activities or exercises. But come spring, I knew that we were going to be playing outside more often between seasons, and I was anticipating that going through the recovery, many games, and much energy exerted in each one.

Over winter vacation I went to the mountain, but I did not ski. My first time back on the mountain was in January that winter. I was a bit nervous. Matt and I took a few easy runs. I went slowly, cautiously, down the slope. It had only been four months since my knee surgery. It held up well despite my leg and knee joint still regaining strength. During February break, I skied every day. I carved between moguls and took the impact going over them. I went off small jumps and landed smoothly. In the gym, I played basketball with everyone. Physically, I was almost back to normal. It seemed like my knee had recovered. There was a month left to the recovery timeline.

Then six months after the surgery, my physical therapist that I had seen over the first few months of that period gave me a performance test. It took place at the orthopedic clinic where I had the surgery. I balanced on my left leg as the clock ticked. I hopped around on that same leg as though doing a one-legged race. I ran sprints between obstacles on the ground, then around cones. She timed me. She measured how far and how high I could jump standing stationary. I did well. She cleared me to return to all high-impact activities. Though I had begun some already, I increased the intensity with those and all the other exercises and high-impact activities.

That year I went to prom. Dressing up suavely, dancing and partying in style seemed exciting. But where it was going to be held and our plans for after the event were up in the air. Some of the boys and I got dates. I was going to prom with Isabel.

About a month beforehand, a girl from another school messaged me and wanted to get together. I thought of Isabel and getting together with her. We still met up that weekend on an island twenty minutes away. I drove there and picked her up at her house. She directed me down the road to a point. There was a small lot for parking and a public pier. Where we parked and most of that section of the island was wooded. We went out on the pier. The water appeared dark and the surface still. It was a brisk day, still cool from winter. Sun broke through between the clouds. Across the sound stood trees along the water's edge and up the bank on which a few houses were built further down and beyond the edge of the land was the bay.

She wanted to live in a modest house, where it has enough space for everyone inside to be together, but small enough so that everyone is crammed in with each other. We were both idealistic but in different ways. Throughout adolescence, some dreams and desires changed from experiences and circumstances. I thought again about Isabel and then her apartment.

We went back to the car and kissed. Ten minutes later another car pulled up next to us. She ducked down in the seat. She peeked through the window. "Oh my god, it's Abigail and Evelyn. We're in the same grade. I know what they'll say at school. 'We saw Sofi with a boy on the island. A moon.' Kiss me."

She perked up in the seat. I backed up and drove out of the lot. Later I dropped her off at her house. The following weekend I went to the mountain and skied. It was the annual reggae festival at the resort. The sun was out, snow was wet, slush in some parts, but smooth. I was lightly clothed. Music played at the base lodge, and people were partying. Beads and bras hung from trees going up the chairlift, even lingerie. We were out on the mountain all day, and then we left the following morning after getting coffee at a cafe. No one was at the house when I walked inside. My parents had gone away for the weekend and perhaps my brother had gone with them. I had some people over that night. We continued the reggae festivities, or rather started them, with music, games, and sports on TV. It might have been our first time at the house upstairs in the living room. We had always gone down in the basement. We ordered food and celebrated into the night.

After school the following day, some of the boys got together and went to a pond near my house. It was part of a land conservation, a large preserve. It had woods and hills and in the center was a big pond. Someone suggested going to the pond after prom. They thought that it was a good idea. I wondered about going to Isabel's apartment afterward. But we decided on going to the pond.

That day some people went there early to set up the tents. I stopped by and helped. They brought other supplies. There was a shack by the edge of the water. It had a chair and a couch, a small porch facing the pond, and a little kitchen that maybe one day had been intact. It used to be a boy scout camp. On a land bridge around the corner connecting one side of the pond with the other was a firepit, and on the far end of the land bridge a stream flowed through and a few planks of wood lay over it to cross. The place was set up and sort of prepared for that night with tables and chairs and tents. Some of us left. I went to the house and started getting ready.

Later, Isabel and I met up at a friend's house near the event. We finished getting ready, and she looked beautiful. We all went to a tavern for dinner. I had a light meal and sparkling water. The prom took place at the country club. It was outside under a large glamorous tent. It had been a warm day, and the weather was mild that night. We paid and then went over to the country club. There were small plates, deserts and beverages spread out on tables that lined parts of the exterior walls. It had a big open space in which most people gathered. We danced for a little while. The music rotated between fast-paced and slow songs. At the end of the event, our ride brought us to the pond and dropped us off. People were already there and many more showed up. The land bridge and the old cabin crowded. I said, "Where is Isabel?" I looked for her. I crossed a small catwalk at the end of the land bridge, those few wooden planks laid out over the stream. It was dark. I stepped on the catwalk between two planks and fell in the water. My phone lay on the ground by the edge of the pond. I picked it up and then dried off and changed clothes. The night was winding down. Isabel had gone to her apartment. I went inside the old cabin and sat on the chair. A girl walked across the room and sat on me in the chair, and then we started to kiss.

    I walked back to the house early that morning before sunrise. Along the way the sky changed color to red and orange and pink. The birds sang softly. I heard them almost like I had as a little boy, calling my name in melody. I made it to the house and went inside up to my bedroom, and then I slept for a couple of hours.

Chapter 43

I focused on school and extracurriculars for the rest of the schoolyear. After my knee injury, the surgery and recovery, I thought that my speed and agility had been affected. My leg had regained its strength to an extent. Right before the injury I had parallel squatted 405 pounds on test day and ran the forty-yard dash in a little over four and a half seconds. My left leg had been my dominant leg. It no longer sprang with each stride like it had. It still did, but not with that same bounce. Instead of doing track and field, I played baseball. For playoffs, I was called up to varsity. Had I played sophomore year, I might have been called up to varsity for playoffs then, but I had run track and got faster for football. The team was good. I was a base runner and still pretty fast after the injury. Maybe no one realized that I had been out for close to half a year. I sat in the dugout, and I enjoyed it. Matt had also been called up. We were involved during games, warmed up and ready to go in, run the bases, get some plate appearances. We went to the state championship game and won.

    Earlier that winter I had bought a ticket to a concert held at the beginning of the summer. As the summer approached, I had thought of it as celebrating the end of the schoolyear and the start of summer, and then that included the championship game too. Esme and I took a bus to South Station in Boston the afternoon of the concert. Isabel met up with us later at the venue. Her father had a condo downtown, and we first stopped at the building and went inside. She set her bag down in one of the extra bedrooms on a pair of bunk beds, then we went into the living room. There was a big couch, a lounge chair with faux fur. Wooden beams stretched across the ceiling to a neat upscale kitchen. I got up and stood before the window wall and balcony and viewed the harbor across the street.

Esme and I walked to the TD Garden. The sun had been out all day and at evening the air was warm in areas of shade. We waited in line for general admission and then went inside. We got right up front next to the stage. Then Isabel joined us. It felt like a fantastic dream. The light show started, and it was the complete spectrum. Rays of light beamed everywhere in all directions, changing colors and motion to the melody of the music, and they almost seemed palpable, as though they were on a higher wavelength, and so were we. The Swedish disc jockey stepped on stage and the place roared. And then, between all the nudging, bouncing and dancing crammed up front, someone reached for my shoulder. It was Esme's sister. We embraced. Isabel's sister was there too. Together all the sisters raved. We split up for a moment, caught up in a sea of people, then grouped back together. We stayed by the stage until the concert ended. The lights turned on. People scrambled. We went outside.

I did not realize when we were inside how crowded it had been in the venue. People were wild outside. We crossed the street and went to a convenience store. There were bags of chips on the ground, the coolers were empty, the slushy machine was messy. We bought water and then grouped up outside.

After returning to the condo, we went to a diner a few blocks away. It was the only restaurant open twenty-four hours a day. We sat at a booth. It must have been about three in the morning. I was tired but still energized and excited from the concert. We ate a late dinner for an early breakfast. And when we got back to the condo, I loved them. We went to bed and fell asleep. Esme and I took an early bus back. The sky cleared. It seemed like a nice day.

On the Fourth of July I went out with Gwynn and some others in his grade and mine. There was a carpool. Someone dropped us off at a house near a lake on the western edge of town. It was not far away. Many people went. We had missed the fireworks but played games. Miles and I made plans to ride longboards.

There were many hills near his house. I had been to a few with him before, and we flew down the road. I was not that good on a longboard. One hill had quite a steep slope. The top was smooth, and then there was a drop-off and a long way to the bottom. I pushed forward and got into a set stance. First there was slight movement to the longboard back and forth going down the top of the hill, then high oscillation after going down the steepest section and riding down the remainder of the hill. I wobbled tremendously on the longboard. I looked back. The hill was behind me, and another sat ahead. We were on a winding road with many slight changes in elevation, hills and sloped sections. Miles came down in his car. He seemed surprised, maybe even impressed. I had never gone down a hill quite that steep on a longboard.

Several times before then we had gone skateboarding and found obstacles, gaps between levels of pavement balancing the topography, and we skated on those. I liked action sports, and he must have too.

Later that summer we went mountain biking. There were many hills and trails. Some were steep in both directions. It was a constant up and down or a jolt going over roots. The effort that it took to get to the top of a hill made it more of a thrill going down, until my front tire went into a stump. I launched airborne over the handlebars. I half flipped and the moment in the air seemed long, then my left shoulder hit the ground first. The next couple days that shoulder throbbed. I got X-rays. My doctor examined the images and then said that I had a type three shoulder separation. He advised against getting surgery on it. I had analgesics all week. I had been working at a restaurant since the previous schoolyear, when my knee had finished recovering, and then with my shoulder injury it was difficult. Its range of motion was limited. The end of my collarbone protruded out a bit from its respective joint connected to the shoulder. I did not play sports in the fall. I started the schoolyear with some adversity.

Chapter 44

Ryan had not played fall sports since middle school, and Miles might not have played one that year either. We enjoyed the start of our senior year, some of the privileges we had, with study halls at the beginning or end of the day, we could have a later start or an earlier end to the day. Anyone who played golf was available more often. They played other sports too, pickup games and practice, adventure and action, but I could not with my shoulder injured. The anticipation to finish that schoolyear was high, and likewise our excitement, enhanced with the late summer weather. We went to a small beach and waterfront on the island that I had gone out to the pier that previous spring. I drove, though I had hoped for someone else to, after enduring the injuries of that previous year. My adolescence had rivered a lot of endurance. We were on the beach, and then more people showed up and we went to a campsite down the coast, atop a steep bank and back in the woods. We played games or stood around the campsite under a high canopy of trees. Then someone said, "Cops are coming!" Most people ran off. Will and I walked along the trail to the lot. Nick was there, and then he drove off wildly. A police officer pulled him over on the bridge going back to the mainland. We went by slowly. Then about a mile down the road a police officer pulled me over. My heart had been racing after going past Nick, and it continued to after getting to the house and going up to bed.

My shoulder seemed even further separated and my brother's ongoing health issues ensued. I went for long walks and jogs on trails through the woods. I liked going by myself. My thoughts cleared, and my mind unwound. But I also enjoyed the company of others when they were available. Ryan and Will joined me sometimes. One day we all went to the pond and hiked around the entire preserve. There were several overgrown trails covered in leaves blending into the landscape throughout the woods. We followed a clearing to the other end, and there was a path that led to another clearing with a fenced-in building on which a large satellite dish spun rapidly or else stilled to a halt. Then we cut back through the woods. We walked not on a trail but instead through all the brush, branches, sticks, and leaves. Ryan wore slippers. They were wet and worn down to the soles. He took them off and went back to the lot barefoot.

I began preparing for college applications. For undergraduate studies, many of the applications were submitted to the universities on a platform through which they all processed the applications. I had taken standardized tests for reading and writing, and math. I scored in the range between six hundred and seven hundred on both but higher on math. I made the honor roll or high honors throughout high school. Our school had advanced placement classes and an international baccalaureate program. I took a couple of AP classes, economics and English. Writing was not my strongest subject then but became one of my most disciplined and focused endeavors. The patterns in numbers clicked with me sooner than the patterns in language and composition. I wrote my essay after school in the afternoon, and then I submitted the applications. Many others submitted theirs at around that time, after fall sports had ended. No teams in our school won a championship that season. I drank a glass of wine to the football team. I had suffered injuries but had been of the last group with athletic discipline before the sports program fostered fewer college athletes.

There was little to do to rehabilitate my shoulder except for exercising the area around the joint lightly. Before that had happened, I went to the mountain with a few others on the football team and the girls. They had stayed at the condo directly across the porch before then, but in the summer we all stayed together. We rode the chairlift and hiked a little way up the mountain and then went to a river flowing down the side of it at a lower elevation and through a valley. Layton suggested going for a swim at the spot, accessed by a hiking trail that was near his place on the western side of the mountain. Water pooled in an area of bedrock wider than the river above and below. I swam across to a boulder on the other side and climbed atop its sloped surface and spread my arms out and up toward the afternoon sun and then dove in the water and came up in the light current, pure, fresh, clear like rain, filtered by granite and minerals. The others sat on a rock ledge along the edge of the river in the sunlight. We caroused at night under the stars. Then after getting back to the house, I went mountain biking.

I did not ski often that winter but went to the mountain a few times. I was often at the house. I spent many days and nights in the basement. I had a glass of wine on occasion, and around that time I started drinking apple cider vinegar diluted with water. I read more and felt brighter, even after turning the clocks back, and with the changing seasons and shorter days. I ran a heater and wore layers. My fingers moved, turning pages. The holistic approach to probiotic supplementation seemed to aid my digestive health, but not quite the digestive disorder that had been mild but pronounced since the start of adolescence or maybe even childhood. With each injury came a fancy for holistic medicine, and all the while it provided a sense of clarity to the gastrointestinal system and in effect the mind, like the last slab of bedrock excavated out the end of the great tunnel.

In February I started working at a nursery. One of my friends Zak did too, and another already had been. We were classmates in last period, and we went to the nursery after school and worked until close at 4:30 p.m. Later in the year they were open until 6:00 p.m. We prepared for the upcoming season that was busiest in the summer and we organized the greenhouses with annuals after they had been assembled in nursery pots. When the baseball season began, our practices started at 5:00 p.m., and we went to them right from work.

I tried to be calculated, and I had to be sharp and meticulous throughout many tasks. There was always something that needed to be worked on and completed, or else something that need to be fixed, organized, or arranged differently, segueing to the next task. After the equinox there was more activity. It was during the busy days of spring when the universities notified applicants on admissions, and I decided on going to the University of New Hampshire for business with a scholarship, and Zak did too for biology.

Sometimes throughout the spring and then the summer when I was not at work or playing sports, I mowed my grandparents' lawn, mostly to say hello. Nana sometimes watched and waved to me from the kitchen window. On the sill sat her tulip bulbs. Papa was somewhere in the house, maybe sitting in his chair. He was 93 years old. I had been mowing their lawn since middle school. Back then he was always at his barbershop. He was there almost everyday until his ninetieth birthday. He had been at Normandy on D Day, then Okinawa, and then in the South Pacific.

I went inside. They paid me when I mowed their lawn, and they left an envelope for me on the counter. "Thank you, Nana," I said.

"Aw, you're welcome, Andrew."

I hugged her and then went to see Papa. He was watching a baseball game in the living room. "Good to see you," he said, patting my shoulder. "Stay for a little while. Flex those biceps."

I sat on the couch and watched the game. I told him that my baseball team was good.

"Yes, good. Strength in accord."

That went to my shoulder. I could play baseball then, and basketball, but could not exert a force with my left arm perpendicular to my body. I could not even do a pushup, other than with just my right arm. I had been in a funk all year since launching off my mountain bike. The springtime in part balanced that gloom a bit.

I went outside after a couple of innings. I got in my car and drove down the street and then to my house. Ryan invited me to his house later. I went over in the morning or afternoon or at night many times throughout the year. It was about a half mile walk from my house. His mother rented it, a single-story house with two bedrooms, and there was an addition to the house behind the garage that was his bedroom for the spring and summer. It had a fireplace, shelves, chairs, a bed, and it was connected to the entryway up a small staircase. There was a sliding door at the bottom of the staircase and in the winter we chilled cans of soda, sports drinks and water outside beside the steps. I had walked to his house through a blizzard. I went up my street and down a few others. I wore my jacket, a hat, gloves and goggles as though I was skiing. Gusts of wind blew in all directions, and heavy snow illuminated by streetlamps dumped down from the sky, sideways, vertical, diagonal, whirling about. The trek was exhilarating. I sat by the fireplace and warmed up and dried off. We drank canned seltzer. Basketball played on the TV. The storm had let up a bit by the time that I walked back to my house. All the trees and rooftops and yards were covered in snow and gleamed in the morning sun the following day.

School for seniors finished early. Everyone had to do an end-of-the-year project. It started in May and lasted for a couple of weeks. Ben and Miles and I were in a group. We helped make public trails in a municipal forest dense with pine trees and evergreens and saw progress every day. Other groups did similar projects. Classes had finished. I graduated with about a 3.5 average. There had been some distress throughout that cumulation. Miles and I went to baseball practice after working on the trails. It was playoffs, and during that period I was scheduled at the nursery on the weekends until the season ended. Again, our team won the state championship game. When we had a banquet after the season ended, I won an award. I placed the trophy in my bedroom.

    A group of us went to a lake in the middle of the summer. It was about three hours north. We arrived in the afternoon. One of Will's relatives owned a lakefront property, and we stayed in the guest house. The first night we went to a party at a sandpit. Ryan hit his head on a metal trailer. All night after that he was a bit delirious, preoccupied and stressed over "the aliens!" I was surprised that we did not see a spacecraft in the sky. There were only stars, constellations, and all the outer space in between. It seemed awe-inspiring, and possibly more so after Ryan and I had some medicine, that is, cannabis, and some of the others too. Then we all went to bed and slept in a tent.

    At sunrise we packed up and went to back to the house. We rode around the lake in a boat all day and we tubed for a while and then stopped the boat and swam and lounged. Some of us went in the water. We each had a foam noodle and a can of beer. We floated around the boat, holding onto the noodle and the can. Cabana music played from the speakers. When we had gotten in the water, the sun was overhead, and then I lay back and looked up and it appeared in the sky far closer to the horizon. We went back to the house and ate bread, meat, cheese, and crackers. For dinner we ate hamburgers, and later that night we played poker. We told Will's cousin that we play basketball a lot. Some of us did most nights, and when there was only three of us, we played games of twenty-one and shot many free throws and scored one basket after another in a continuous often even sequence. Otherwise, I read in the basement when I got to the house, I still did puzzles, drew, or played videogames.

It was another nice day in the morning. Dew covered the grass and areas in the sun shone lighter, like the undersides of leaves. We took the boat to an island after going to the store and stopping for breakfast. On it was a mountain, a large rock face, a few cliff divers. We moored the boat and stepped ashore. There was a golf course between the mountain and the water that wrapped around a shaded cove on a strip of land. We did not play a round of golf, but we walked along the pathway of one hole and checked out the fairway and the green. The conditions seemed pristine, and the course was secluded, out on an island in the middle of the lake. Sunlight lay on the rockface and trickled through fluttering leaves to the ground. The grass glowed in the clearings, and the water did too, rippling out to the other end of the lake that could be seen facing some directions.

We got in the boat and went back to the house. We cleaned and organized our quarters before leaving the next day. That night we went out to the waterfront and on the dock under the clear sky and stars for a moment. The night air felt light and slightly warm. We set off on the road in the morning.

Chapter 45

I arrived at the college dorm room first and set my bags down on the bottom bunk. There was a top bunk and bed above and a half bunk on the other side of the room with a bed only on top. I took the bed on the bottom bunk, then unloaded the car and made my bed, unpacked my clothes, and sat down for a moment. One of my roommates, Alex, arrived next. I helped him unload and get situated. Then we went outside and walked through the campus. We followed a trail through a wooded area and sat on a log beside a gully. The streets, lots, and unloading areas had begun to fill early and bustled throughout the day. We went back to the room and our other roommate Jake had arrived. We introduced ourselves and helped him unpack and then went out back to the basketball court and tried to find our dorm room window. It was on the eighth floor, and it was a small room for three people. We spotted it up there, then went up and met many of our floormates and some others on the floors below. Among them were Taylor and Kevin who lived in the room across the hall, Caleb who lived in the room next door, and there was John, Leo, Dino, Tim, Griffin, Bella, Ava, Liz, Amy, Richelle, Mel, Katie, Hailey, and Emilie too. We were on the eastern wing on the top floor of the most populated dorm hall.

We went out every night the first week of classes, after going over the syllabi, familiarizing ourselves with the campus, locating each building in which our classes were held, and eating at the dining halls. It could get rowdy along the row of fraternity houses and by the apartment complexes on the same street or nearby. We went to some parties and gatherings around there and hung out in our room or the one across the hall. The rooms were maybe about two hundred square feet. They could fill up quickly. My bed, being the bottom bunk, acted as a couch when others hung out in our room.

The following week, the nocturnal bustle settled down a bit. It was not that the curriculums picked up in demand after the first week, but assignments were due, there were quizzes, and material for the first set of exams were being covered and new assignments introduced. People had settled in and focused on classes. I took economics, business, philosophy, and calculus.

I had a class with my roommate Alex and Caroline who I had known in high school. It was economics, and we had it in a lecture hall across the street from our dorm building. I helped him through the assignment problems and studied with Caroline. We went over the principles of microeconomics in detail, and after taking macroeconomics in high school, each principle and concept could be compared, inspire free associations between fields, and be explored more by delving deeper into the materials and the mind. One side of the cube is economic behavior, and there are many squares on each side that move, rotate, twist and turn to reach a balance all around the cube, each side in equilibrium to its organization, and the cube is the world, its surfaces are the present, and its volume enlarges or reduces with respect to its equilibrium. I thought that there could be formed a new institution, one that really describes consciousness, what in part makes up the volume of the cube and directs the invisible hand or its concept in not only economic theory, but innovation and insight too, an output of consciousness, rotating, twisting and turning the squares to reach a balance on each side and an equilibrium as a whole.

After the third week of college, my mind spun. Intellect interweaved with stress, and it was not exactly from classes. I had gone out in the wooded area behind the dorm at night to have cannabis with my roommate. Two others were already there sitting on a log, and then we sat down. Moments later we were caught with cannabis. We rode in a cruiser to the police station. They handcuffed us to a bench and after sitting like that for a few hours we got our paperwork and walked across campus back to the dorm. We learned that that had happened to many others too, and they went through the government. We were on edge for a little while. My mind and perhaps the microbiota directing consciousness did not rest after that. I thought that I had stomach problems. The distress influenced my focus.

I had met Daniela in business class. She may have realized the distress. I walked with her after class. We went to her building and played ping pong in the lobby. She was good. I loosened up. We went back and forth playing "Table tennis." Then, "Game point." And then, "Let's go!" We went upstairs.

Her building was somewhat new and so was her room. I had learned that mine was of the raunchiest on campus. There may have been clothes scattered around. Most of the rooms had the same or a similar layout. She made her bed. It was five o'clock. I walked across campus and later ate dinner at the dining hall.

We had to complete twenty-four hours of community service, and we started on those and completed the hours in three consecutive weekends. I went on Sundays. They began at 8:00 a.m. and lasted until 4:00 p.m., and it all had to be completed at a facility twenty minutes away in the county. We got a ride there and split and stacked wood all day. I made lunch at the dining hall the night before and brought that to eat during the break. For breakfast I ate a bar made of grains. The seasons changed over that period. Daylight hours reduced and it was almost dark when we arrived back at the dorm. We then ate dinner. I drank a cup of coffee after. It seemed to direct internal energy downward, meanwhile uplifting the mind. I had completed the assignments due at the beginning of the following week and caught up on studies. I helped others with homework, sometimes in my room and across the hall. They often had sports playing on their TV.

Daniela suggested going in a sauna. I later stayed inside one for an hour over winter break, and it exercised body, mind, internal energy, endurance. Water seeped through the pores, along with toxins, heavy metals, compounds of a high and low pH. I emerged feeling fresh. It was not until later, over a period when I went in saunas more often, that I discovered a holistic approach to reaching equilibrium in gut health and that prompted part of a book.

We walked through the woods. The past flashed kaleidoscopically, and the world shone in new light, dazzling, fractally serene.

I went to Boston over the weekend in the middle of fall. I took the subway into Cambridge and met up with Ryan. He led me past Harvard Yard. I got excited. We went a few blocks further inland and stopped at his room first, then ate nearby. We got a ride to his teammates' apartment and later, after we went to a few parties, I slept on their couch. Ryan stopped by in the morning. We walked back to his room, then had lunch in Back Bay. There was a large, round grill in the center of the dining area where the food that we had picked out from stations along the wall was cooked and prepared. We brought our plates back to the table and ate, then got up for seconds, then thirds. There was one fee per patron. Ryan paid the bill, and I left a tip on the table. We went outside, and then I walked to the train station and boarded the train.

Our first break was in November. I took an evening train to the house on the last day of classes that week. Papa fell down the stairs in his house the day before Thanksgiving. He had osteoporosis and was in critical condition at the hospital. My parents and relatives and I were worried, distressed. I went back to school on Sunday; that Thursday he passed away.

The funeral was held the following Friday. I went to the house the night before after my last class for the day. We got ready in the morning. I was downstairs when the phone rang, and my mother was upstairs when she answered. Nana had suddenly become ill. Then she was rushed to the hospital. I heard my mother say, "This is an effing nightmare!"

We went to Papa's funeral. Visitation was held in the morning and after a couple of hours inside we went to the cemetery. I helped lift the casket. It was lowered into the ground. We all cried and then left afterward. My parents dropped me off at the train station. They went to the hospital to see my grandmother.

It was then finals week at school. I finished every exam in two days. I did well on them and even made the Dean's list. I got on the train and went back to the house in the evening and went to bed later that night and then saw some friends the next day in the afternoon. I did not mention Papa's passing or Nana's being in the hospital.

My mother received updates every day from the hospital on her mother's condition. Early the following month, she passed away.

It was one month after her husband had, starting on the day of his funeral. He was 94, and she was 81. God bless them.

I was sullen after their passing. I told Alex and Jake, "That may be equilibrium. A combined composition of microbiota."

"I'm so sorry man."

"Thank you."

We all got into a routine, learned our schedules, and then each other's. Our dorm room was small. We were in it often, between classes and on the weekends, and so were other people who lived in the building, and sometimes other people around campus. Occasionally, we even had people from high school staying with us. The door was always open, and it became kind of a community room. It started one night after dinner. Alex, Jake and I moved some furniture around the room.

"Let's put that there, slide this here. There, turn that around. Now put the tv on top of the dresser, good, and the chair on the bureau. Like this, facing the tv. Let's move the bunkbed against the wall. Beside the window, right like this. That little space underneath the bunkbed. Got the desk. The fan. A chair. It's a space to lounge. And look, at all, the room we have now."

"Some men have two first names, Peter Kevin."

"Just turning simple things into brilliant things."

Like arranging simple squares into complex cubes. We created a creative space. After rearranging the furniture, natural light streamed in, and we had space for a chair atop a bureau, more space in the center of the room to play basketball on a miniature hoop or to lean back in the chairs at our desks.

With the extra floor space, we had more seating in our room. We watched tv, I felt a bit pained. I searched for inspiration, intrigued by a documentary of Shep, a legend to me. How quickly my spirits were lifted. When writing, I sometimes slacked at the end of a project, like letting out line at the end of a catch. It is a sense of relief and moment of ease. The momentum may be influenced by the tide, by a certain planetary moment of inertia. I finished my paper quickly. He said that I write, and I'm good, better than usual.

A bead of sweat dripped down the side of my cheek. *So my writing's unusual?*

I learned how to code and then delved into the Information Age and parts of the internet matrix, a melting pot of data, memory, information, and systems. I made a website and later made one to maintain as a platform for my writing.

Toward the end of the semester, after finishing most of the schoolwork, we went on a short field trip. We all boarded a big boat and went out onto the water. We collected some samples of seawater at various locations and depths with our professor that we then researched and studied further in the laboratory. Perhaps we probed climatic problems, sea levels and temperatures rising, some of the effects on habitats and the adaptations of marine organisms. On the field trip, we had set out on the boat from a part of the coastline enclosed like a nest. Narrowly connected to the mainland, it jutted out into the water of an estuary just inland from the ocean. It was a wildlife refuge, a sanctuary for birds, and there were hiking trails throughout and around the tip of the land.

In the fall of sophomore year, I went hiking along the trails. I either started along the north end or cut south through a clearing, then looped around the western edge, up a hill, over logs, down a ledge, all along the water's edge. Small waves rolled in and over stones where trees had once stood. The sun shone throughout the point and out atop the water from which a warm breeze rolled in.

I lived in an apartment with Taylor and Jake. Alex lived across the parking lot with Tim. We went hiking on the weekends up north by the White Mountains when the fall season started. The deciduous trees had vibrant foliage. Looking out from a south-facing overlook just below the summit stood a range of mountains on either side and between them sat a valley overlaid with sunlight that curved out toward the horizon. Carved down the middle was a road and above lay blue sky and a couple clouds. We planned to go with Bella, Richelle, and Amy. Alex and Huey came on a weekend when there were strong gusts of wind at the summit and dense clouds and fog surrounded us and the landscape and the sky.

The clocks turned back. Season and memory blurred and blended. Over winter break I played hockey. I skied. It blurred. And consciousness ebbed, as though to the universe.

It fogged. The moonlight dimmed. And I gasped for air.

The piano played.

Second movement.
Then later at night, a turning moment.
Sea birds squawked, above, below, left, and right.
The sequence stilled. Dimensions darkened. And then there was light.